THE
INSPIRATION
FACTOR

*How to Tap into People's Dreams and
Create a Culture of Passion and Loyalty*

FOREWORD BY
Laurie Beth Jones, Bestselling Author of *Jesus* CEO

THE
INSPIRATION
FACTOR

*How to Tap into People's Dreams and
Create a Culture of Passion and Loyalty*

TERRY BARBER
WITH PAT SPRINGLE

Edited by Renee Chavez
Formatted by Anne McLaughlin, Blue Lake Design, Dickinson, Texas.

Scriptures marked NIV are taken from the HOLY BIBLE: NEW INTERNATIONAL VERSION.® © 1973, 1978, 1984 by International Bible Society. Used by permission of Zondervan Publishing House. All rights reserved.

Published in the United States by Baxter Press, Friendswood, Texas.

ISBN: 978-1-888237-79-5

Publisher's note: Stories in this book, except for the author's personal stories, are taken from conversations with clients and friends. To protect their anonymity, most of the names and some details have been changed.

Teach . . . and hopefully they will learn.
Lead . . . and they may follow.
Inspire . . . and they will never be same.

CONTENTS

Acknowledgments

A few very special people have impacted me profoundly, though I have never met them in person. It's the words they put into print that have inspired me. Every year for the past twenty years, I've read Dale Carnegie's classic book *How to Win Friends and Influence People*. A few years ago, C. S. Lewis challenged me with the thought that pain is "God's megaphone"[1] to get our attention. It was Lewis's authentic approach to pain that first allowed me to turn the most difficult time of my life into a defining moment.

But my life is full of passion and contentment mostly because it contains a rich portfolio of *relationships*. To the people with whom I "do life," I owe much gratitude.

To my daughters, Brittany, Lindsey, Tommee, and Amanda — thank you for giving me the freedom to speak the principles in this book into your lives. In the process, I actually learned more than I taught.

To my mom and dad, thank you for inspiring me to pursue dreams that require my God-given, unique gifts and talents. You never gave up on me.

To my three little sisters and younger brother, who at least acted interested when I tried out new speeches on you as an aspiring public speaker at the age of ten — thanks, guys. I'm more than grateful.

I'm also very grateful for people who didn't always heap praise upon me. Instead, they loved me enough and were courageous enough to speak hard truths to me. One of these trusted friends is my good friend Laurie Beth Jones. After a day of whining to her about what a victim I was of some difficult times, she quickly reminded me of the truth about who I was. Immediately, I stopped playing the role of a victim. Laurie Beth, thank you for the pep talk!

To Pat Springle, who helped make this book move from just an idea to reality, I'm very thankful. I appreciate your diligence, your partnership—but above all, your friendship. My life is truly richer because of you.

To my good friend Larry Bone—you and I have been doing life together for thirty-seven years. Though there are only ten years of difference in our ages, I'm convinced I will never catch up to your insight into people's hearts and your ability to bring out the best in them. As my youth leader in 1971, you saw potential in me that I certainly didn't see in myself. All your life, Larry, you have pursued a vision much bigger than yourself. You have enjoyed the friendship of many people, but your greatest reward will come when heaven reveals the untold numbers of people, like me, that you have inspired.

My life has been molded and catapulted by several other inspiring people. Three of them are my longtime friends Jerry Riggs, Scott Kimbro and Jamie Wright. Jerry, I'm grateful that God put you into my life. Scott, thank you for always reminding me that all things do work together for good, and Jamie, your enthusiasm is contagious and I am a better person because of you.

One of the blessings of my job is that I've been able to watch some of my clients create inspiring cultures in their companies and organizations. I thank each of them for their example: Cindy Eller, Laurel Dibrog, and Candace Johnson have done a masterful job at the Roswell Park Cancer Institute in Buffalo, New York. Paola Werstler and Sabrina Gonzales have worked to inspire their staff at the Arizona Cancer Center. I've also seen the powerfully positive impact of Rosemary Gruber and her husband, Don, at the University of Minnesota Cancer Center; and Carol Jefferson and her husband, David, at the Holden Cancer Center at the University of Iowa. Finally, Jon Huntsman and his team at the Huntsman Cancer Institute inspire me every time I'm around them, especially my friend and client Heather Levan. I love these people.

I also want to say a special thank you to Chip Grizzard and my co-workers at Grizzard Communications, Inc. who have given me the opportunity to put into practice these life-enhancing principles. What a privilege it is to work for a company with such high integrity.

Finally, I want to say thank you to my wife, Debbi, who never grows tired of seeing the best in me. Debbi, you, too, have created an inspirational culture—at work *and* in our home. I'm indebted to you.

FOREWORD

"Culture trumps strategy." This simple statement, made by a CEO of a billion dollar organization that I was coaching, has stayed with me for years. No matter what brilliant plans you may have for your team or organization, or even family, if there is not a culture of authenticity, and loyalty, those plans will never materialize.

Terry Barber is one of those rare people who is a force of nature. His exuberance for life, and genuine love for people, belies a brilliant strategic mind that has been honed in one of the toughest markets there is: raising money for youth organizations. Now he has expanded that into various money making enterprises, all without losing his soul.

Simply put, if Terry believes in something, everyone around him eventually will too. What excites me about this book is that someone has taken a natural gifting of inspiration and enthusiasm, and broken it down into parts that other people can learn to emulate.

Whether it is learning to be true to oneself, which is the beginning of authenticity, or learning to appreciate and value the benefits of great storytelling, this book brings it all together in simple, easy to understand language, filled with real life examples.

I hope you have the pleasure of meeting Terry Barber one day. Once you get in his orbit, you begin yourself to spin a little faster, believe in yourself a little more, see the sunshine instead of the shadow, and laugh your deepest laugh.

If you don't ever meet Terry personally, the very least you can do is get this book, and read it. It is like liquid nitrogen on paper . . .

shake it up in your own life, and watch your results explode into joy, and delight, and beauty.

I call him "T-Ray" for a reason. He is bigger than life.

Read this work, and you will be too.

By Laurie Beth Jones
Author of Jesus, CEO; The Path; Jesus Life Coach
July 18, 2008

INTRODUCTION: REDEFINING INSPIRATION

"Keep away from people who try to belittle your ambitions. Small people always do that, but the really great make you feel that you, too, can become great." — Mark Twain

If I were to ask you to come up with some synonyms for the word inspiration, what would you tell me? Stimulation, no doubt. *Encouragement,* or perhaps *influence,* in a positive sense. The number one answer I would hear, though, would be *motivation.* Most folks would say inspiration and motivation are one and the same.

But over the years, I've seen a sometimes subtle, but often significant, distinction between motivation and inspiration. Motivation provides an incentive for people to act in certain ways, but for reasons that can be noble . . . *or* selfish. They may even act out of fear. *Motivation,* then, can either be positive or negative, productive or destructive.

Inspiration, on the other hand, is always good, always positive. It focuses on people's deepest and noblest desires. Inspiration is, in fact, an "exalting influence."[1]

Definitions matter.

Most business books and seminars focus on motivation, and they often encourage executives and managers to use the full range of incentives to produce motivation down the corporate ladder. And sometimes these leaders succeed. They take those "motivational principles" back to the workplace, and their employees are, indeed, motivated. They're doing an outstanding job!

But motivation can easily be tarnished by manipulation, fear, and demands, and the consequences can devastate people rather than encourage them. Yes, their leader may have motivated them, but who knows what his or her methods were. Dangling carrots offering short-term reward? Threats and ultimatums? Whatever the case, these people's motivation is short-lived, because their leader only scratched the surface.

MOTIVATION V. INSPIRATION: A CASE IN POINT

My relationship with my father taught me a lot about the differences between motivation and inspiration. When I was a boy, my dad used three forms of inducement on me: positive motivation, manipulative motivation, and inspiration. Two of these were counterproductive.

More times than I care to remember, when I brought my report card home from school, my father would study it, give me one of those looks that said it all, sigh deeply, and say, "Son, this just won't do. You're living *way below* your potential. You've got to figure out a way to apply yourself and do better—a *lot* better." Positive motivation. And my father meant well with his "do better" speech, but this method of motivation never produced long-term positive change. Still, it would work for a time, because his positive motivation was often backed with a threat, spoken or not. I was well aware that if I didn't do better in the next term, I'd experience severe consequences. I had five siblings—two brothers and three sisters—and there were no favorites when it came to Dad's administration of consequences. We were all very familiar with what we would simply refer to as "the belt." Fear is a powerful motivator, but it's a lousy source of inspiration. (I'm not claiming, by the way, that I didn't ever deserve "the belt" from time to time. I'm just explaining that, while it definitely "motivated" me and manipulated me to enhance my performance, it certainly didn't *inspire* me!)

But on many mornings, Dad's attitude and actions inspired me. He would stand in the kitchen as he made his coffee, singing and clapping to the rhythm of Tennessee Ernie Ford. Then, as he drove me to school, he would ask me questions such as, "Son, what are you looking forward to today?" and, "How are you going to make a difference today?" These questions, and the smile on his face as he asked them, made me want to be like him — *inspired* me to be like him. They also assured me that my father believed in me — and I ate it up! Those times with my dad made me a better man.

An example of true inspiration occurred the day my dad took me to work with him. At the time, his customers were lumberyard owners and managers. I'll always remember him introducing me to his customers, all through the day. He taught me to shake hands assertively, with a good, firm grip. He told me to look his customers in the eye, and say my name loud and clear. That day my dad inspired me! I remember thinking, *I want to be able to meet people like my dad does,* and *I'd love to have people like me as much as they like him.*

Dad did more that day than just motivate me for the duration of the workday. He actually tapped into my dreams (to impact people), giving me a vision, not just today, but for my future. In fact, *every* time my dad inspired me, he had a lasting impact. That's how inspiration works, and that's the difference between it and motivation. Leaders who gen-

> *Leaders who genuinely inspire others do so by tapping into their dreams, eliciting the best from them, and ultimately changing their lives.*

uinely *inspire* others do so by tapping into their dreams, eliciting the best from them, and ultimately changing their lives. Perhaps these leaders have an intuitive knack for inspiring those around them — or they may have developed this skill through years of training, trial, and error, as my dad did. Either way, it is the *inspiration factor* that produces more positive transformation — in teams, companies, families, and with clients/customers — than any other leadership trait.

LESSONS LEARNED — THE HARD WAY

Many years after that day at Dad's workplace, with college, graduate school, and several years of work behind me, I was asked to supervise a group of interns for a year. I was thirty-one, and it was my first management role. I'd taken courses in management, I'd read books about business, and I'd had countless conversations about the best ways to lead, manage, and motivate people. But when the day arrived that my first four interns walked through the door, I reverted back to the "live up to your potential" kind of motivation that my father used on me. I had learned to use positive words — but in a negative, threatening way: "Live up to your potential . . . *or you'll have to answer for it!*"

As the months went by, some patterns surfaced. Sometimes my interns worked really hard, but often I could tell that their hearts just weren't in it. From time to time, their minds would drift from the tasks assigned to them, and a couple of them were habitually late for meetings. Almost every day, I kicked into my corrective mode:

"What's the problem? Let me see your daily planner. You've got to maximize your day!"

"Repeat after me, with enthusiasm: *'We are fired up. We love our work. We are world changers!'*"

"We've got work to do! Our mission is much more important than we are, and we have the chance to *make a difference!* If you don't get going, there are other people right behind you who are waiting to take your job."

"I need you to be here on time — and the second you get here, you'd better be fired up!"

To be honest, they responded to me exactly as I had responded to my father's "live up to your potential" talk. Each time I met with one of them concerning personal performance, he or she would do better — for a day or two — but then revert to old habits.

By this time, I managed several groups of interns, and invariably, in every group, one of them would do everything I asked — with a smile on her face! Soon, it dawned on me why teachers have "pets" in their classes, because I did too! My delight in my "pets" caused even more conflict in my relationships with those who, I was sure, needed a "butt-kicking" every few days.

My experience overseeing those groups of interns was both exhilarating and frustrating. When they responded to me, I saw the light in their eyes, because they connected their talents and ambitions with a transcendent purpose, and I was thrilled! But their excuses for their failures and their whining about every imaginable thing just about drove me crazy. It seemed that the more I endeavored to inspire them, the more they made excuses and whined. I tried all kinds of motivational techniques, but nothing seemed to work. I wanted their hearts to be captured by the vision of making a difference, so that nothing else mattered. A few got it, but many didn't. I kept trying to pump them up, but they leaked — really badly. I felt like a colossal failure.

My frustration drove me to look for answers, and at that point, I found a new book that had just hit the market: *The 7 Habits of Highly Effective People,* by Stephen R. Covey. As I read the book, one directive stood out as if it were written in neon lights: "Seek first to understand, then to be understood." I realized that the approach I had taken with the interns had been far too external, and to be honest, my interaction with them had been designed to pressure them into meeting my goals. I had failed miserably to touch their hearts. Gradually, I started to make changes in how I related to them.

One of the interns who drove me crazy was Craig, a laid-back, easygoing young man from Fort Worth, Texas. Over and over again, I tried to get him to do better by pointing out his flaws and telling him he was performing below his potential. After a while (and I suspect it didn't take long), he dreaded to see me coming. But with a new insight about inspiration, I took a different approach. I sat down with Craig and asked him about his goals, his dreams, and his ambitions. I invited dialogue and discovery: "Craig, tell me what attracted you to this intern position." He seemed a bit hesitant at first, but soon, out of his mouth spilled clearly articulated dreams and aspirations — which I never knew existed.

"Terry," he said, "I've always been a little bashful, and I hoped this role would help me become more courageous and confident in connecting with people." That single statement melted my heart, and it showed me how badly I had missed the opportunity to shape Craig's life. In an instant, my thinking, my assumptions, and my process of relating to Craig changed. I could tap into his dreams and genuinely inspire him.

With a new vision for my role as a manager, I met with the other three interns. Each of them shared their dreams and desires, and I learned that each of them came to the program for very different reasons. Now I could tailor my interactions with each of them to tap into their unique, internal engines of motivation—and it made all the difference in the world!

Today, more than twenty years later, Craig Beckett tells people that I played an important role in his life. I can't tell you what that means to me, especially because I had failed so profoundly in my early relationship with him. But Craig wasn't the only one who was transformed. I had envisioned my role as the Master Disciplinarian, tasked with forcing people to work hard with enthusiasm, but now my task was to connect their hearts to the mission, to uncover their desires, encourage their dreams, and find the best way for them to fulfill those dreams in the organization.

Now my task was to connect their hearts to the mission, to uncover their desires, encourage their dreams, and find the best way for them to fulfill those dreams in the organization.

Frankly, there wasn't always a good match between an intern's dreams and the organization's mission. As my perception of my role changed, my goal wasn't to force square pegs into round holes. Instead, I tried to find the best fit for people, and we celebrated when they found a new place where they could thrive, even if it meant their working for a different employer—and celebration is a lot more fun than resentment!

Since those days, I've had many interns and scores of direct and indirect reports. I certainly can't say that every single one of them adores me, but I have had the privilege to hear from many of them that I was a source of inspiration and encouragement, and many have told me that I made a huge difference in the direction of their lives.

"INSPIRATION BEGINS AT HOME"

The insights I learned with my interns and the new direction I adopted for managing people had a compelling effect on my relationship with my three daughters. When they were little, before the lights came on for me, I gave them the "live up to your potential" treatment that I had given to the interns — with very similar results. If you ask Brittany (the oldest of the three) about my parenting style when she, Lindsey, and Tommee were little girls, she would tell you that every week, I demanded that they write their goals and post them on the refrigerator. (Try to picture that scene when they were seven, five, and three years old!) Then I'd review their goals and hold them accountable. I cringe when I think about my behavior, though they seemed to have gotten through it without too much damage. They now tease me about it — regularly!

But when I began changing my corporate management style, I started the transition at home too. I started asking the girls about their hopes and dreams, and I delighted in their heartfelt motivation to achieve their own goals, not just to comply with mine. Today, my relationship with them is far different than it would have been if I hadn't learned those lessons — and I am very, very grateful. They know that no one is more committed to their personal goals and dreams than me. And that inspires them.

THE SEVEN PRINCIPLES

I've had the great privilege of rubbing shoulders with men and women who inspired me; now I want to inspire others. If you've picked up this book, it's fair to say that you, too, want to be someone who inspires and celebrates courage in other people's lives every day. Your noble desire is one of the most challenging — and fulfilling—pursuits in life. How better to achieve life fulfillment than by inspiring another to greatness?

And here's the good news: though we come from different backgrounds with widely varied experiences, and our personalities differ in many ways, every person is uniquely equipped to inspire others.

Years ago, I began my career as an inspirational speaker to the toughest demographic group in America: teenagers. Three days each week on as many as three different campuses a day, I walked into auditoriums to inspire and motivate five hundred to five thousand teens. My goal was to help them find self-esteem in personal values and make their decisions based on timeless wisdom, rather than simply perform on a competitive team or just make good grades. It was during this time that I observed firsthand the truth in the saying "birds of a feather flock together."

Though the large-group presentations always seemed to go well, the break-out sessions were by far more difficult. Yet it was there where I learned how to inspire people even in the most hostile environments. Many times I had to face the cynical and critical attitudes of a group of students classified as "high risk." In the crucible of these difficult experiences, I learned some basic principles of inspiration that work in every market, culture, and demographic—even for high-risk people. Since that time, I've used these same principles to inspire employees, clients, customers, and donors, with my bosses, my children, interns, and friends. They'll work for you too.

In this book, I will present seven principles that are critical in effectively inspiring others. As you explore them, you will learn how to identify the embers in others—and how to fan those embers into flames of passion, loyalty, and excellence. These principles work in any context (with individuals, teams, divisions, or multinational corporations), so even if no one else in your organization "gets it," *you* can take the initiative and apply them—with outstanding results—to those under your leadership.

The seven principles are:

Principle #1: Be Authentic

Principle #2: Connect with Others' Dreams

Principle #3: See in Others the Abilities They Don't See in Themselves

Principle #4: Speak with Credibility

Principle #5: Inspire with Great Stories — Yours and Theirs

Principle #6: Help People Live on Purpose

Principle #7: Create a New Culture

Before we get very far, though, I want to be sure that we redefine the word *inspiration*. Too often, inspiration is seen as an *act*, and often, one that is merely fluff — cheerleading devoid of substance — but in these pages, you'll see that inspiration is a *character trait*, an invaluable leadership characteristic that includes insights, skills, humility, and courage. It's not enough to pat people on the back occasionally and say, "You're great!" or "That's awesome!" That's a one-time act — that we may repeat over and over. We can do better than that — *much* better. Inspiration is the developed *ability* and *commitment* to connect people's deepest motivations with their sharpest skills. When we inspire those around us, we develop strong relationships based on loyalty,

> *When we inspire those around us, we develop strong relationships based on loyalty, not manipulation or threats.*

not manipulation or threats. Creating this kind of culture takes intention and effort, but it's worth it to see people thrive.

In his insightful book *Good to Great*, author and professor Jim Collins describes several levels of leadership, including "Competent Managers," "Effective Leaders," and what he calls "Level 5 Executives." Effective Leaders, he wrote, "catalyze commitment to and vigorous pursuit of a clear and compelling vision, stimulating higher performance standards." A worthy goal. But a Level 5 Executive, wrote Collins, "builds enduring greatness [in the organization] through a paradoxical blend of personal humility and professional will."[2]

Ego, drive, and charisma cause many leaders to focus only on their own goals, instead of the dreams of others. But humility triggers the Level 5 manager to look beyond him- or herself and care passionately about others around the office—and it is essential for leaders who inspire.

Of course, in writing about the Level 5 Executive, Collins was talking about top executives in major companies. But the same "paradoxical blend" can be developed in leaders at *any* level: in companies, nonprofit organizations, churches—and families. All of us bring particular abilities to our reporting relationships, and we can all learn to inspire people. It may be easier for some than others, but everyone can learn what I learned and have the kind of influence on others that I had on Craig, my children, and many others—as long as we keep our definitions straight.

INSPIRATION AND "WINDSPIRATION"

In his book, Collins also wrote that, often, companies bring in high-powered visionaries to lead a company turnaround. The corporate board wants quick, decisive action, and these high-profile execs promise to deliver. Yet their chief attribute isn't their ability to help others succeed; they're all about their own stellar reputations. People around such a leader only serve to make *his* vision a reality; he doesn't concern himself at all with theirs. Collins calls this type of leader a "genius and a thousand helpers."[3] I know exactly the kind of impact this brand of leader has on others, because I've seen it up close.

Not long after graduate school, I went to work for a woman who was known as one of the nation's most respected leaders. She communicated a compelling vision with plenty of emotion. In fact, she was one of the most gifted speakers I've ever heard—colorful, challenging, and entertaining. Because of her reputation, I was certain she could mentor me and that, under her leadership, I would become an equally powerful leader and speaker. Soon, however, my illusions were shattered. The more time I spent with her, the more I found that she was all fluff, no substance. In other words, she was full of "windspiration," not inspiration. In fact, those who spent too much time with her were actually *drained* of inspiration. Why? Because her "tools of the trade" were selfishness and manipulation. She didn't give a rip about me or anyone else who worked for her. I was supposed to be one of her protégés, but in reality I was just one of the cogs in her machine.

This nationally known leader was so poor at understanding and inspiring people that she had to acquire new staff and board members every few years. Each previous group left when they realized that she was an empty shell. Worse, she had no real relationships.

One of the indelible images in my memory was the day she called me into her office to meet her husband's tailor. "Terry," she said, "I want to have a new suit made for you. Would you like that?"

"Sure, I guess so," I answered, not knowing whether to be honored or offended. "What patterns and colors do I get to pick from?"

"Oh," she quickly replied, "I've already picked the color for you."

I was really surprised. "Really? What color is it?"

She smiled and said, "Black. You can wear it on many different occasions." I thought it was strange that she was more excited than I was about this tailor-made suit.

It all came together one day when she introduced me to someone at a national news network as her driver. *Hmmm . . . black suit, driver . . .* Suddenly, it dawned on me that I looked like a professional chauffeur in that suit! She had often told me, "Terry, I'm going to make you my right-hand man!" Now it all made sense. Being her "right-hand man" had nothing to do with grooming me to become an effective speaker or leader; it meant I was her servant!

This took place while my boss and I were in Cincinnati. As soon as I realized how corrupt and duplicitous my employer really was, I turned in my resignation, took a cab to the airport, and caught the next plane back home to New Orleans.

How many times have we seen this kind of selfish, destructive behavior in corporate America? In every field, the loss of good employees is at epidemic proportions. In the fund-raising industry, the average gift officer's tenure is down to eighteen months. Though some are simply seeking new and better opportunities, most leave because they are being treated the same way I was.

Throughout my career, I've been around a number of leaders who offered nice platitudes but didn't take the time to get to know me and find out what drives me. Consequently, they didn't make much of a dent in my life. But I've also had the privilege of knowing — and being known by — a few wonderful leaders whose ability to inspire me changed my life.

When I was a bashful, awkward, annoying teenager living in New Orleans, my church youth worker was a young man named Larry Bone. As I think back on that time in my life, it's hard to imagine that Larry saw anything worth affirming in me, but he did. I distinctly remember one particular conversation, when he looked me in the eye and said, "Terry, I can see that you really care about people, and you want to make a difference in their lives." Wow! That desire was certainly there, but it was buried deep in the muck of adolescent insecurities. But Larry wasn't through: "I think you have the potential to be a terrific communicator."

Me? I wondered as I looked around. *Is he talking to somebody else?*

No, he was talking to me. He saw latent abilities that I'd never dreamed were there.

He saw latent abilities that I'd never dreamed were there.

One day, Larry took me aside and told me solemnly, "Terry, there's more to life than you're living now. God has something for you that's much bigger than anything you've ever dreamed possible, and I believe you're going to achieve it. Do you want me to help you find out what it is?"

I jumped at his offer: "You bet I do!"

In my relationship with Larry, he never made me feel like a rec-lamation project. Even when I seemed to have very little to offer (which, looking back, was all day, every day), he treated me with respect. And Larry was the picture of humility. He never tried to be someone he wasn't. He often laughed and said, "I'm just a country boy from Arkansas," as he gave everything he had to every person around him.

Recently I told a friend about Larry's impact on me. "When was the last time you talked to him?" he asked. I had actually spoken with Larry the previous week. We've remained great friends through all these decades, marriages, children, jobs, and the other ups and downs in life. People like Larry make great friends.

Whether he realized it or not, Larry successfully applied the very principles of inspiration that we will examine in this book. As a result, he forged a genuine, lifelong relationship with me, and I will always be loyal as a friend.

Whether your focus is on customers, clients, donors, employees, family, or friends, the principles of inspiration produce a deep, long-lasting sense of loyalty. In our fast-paced, fragmented, often shallow society, people long for authentic relationships that go below the surface and tap into hidden or neglected dreams. Building these re-lationships is our biggest challenge and our highest privilege. But it can be done. And it begins with examining our priorities.

PRIORITIES

Whether we realize it or not, we organize our lives around just a few, most important relationships. Why? Because only a few people truly capture our hearts and shape our schedules. It is precisely these people whom we can—and should—seek to in-spire, spending a disproportionate part of our emotional capital on them, and them alone. From time to time we may get out of balance and try to spread ourselves too thin. On these occasions, we need to change course and reset our priorities. It's not our job to inspire everybody everywhere.

So, who merits our concentrated investment? At the center of the target are our families, our closest friends, and those who report to us at work. Every now and then, we may carve out some time to devote attention to acquaintances or people on the street, but in so doing we'd better not neglect the people in the center! They deserve our prime hours, our best efforts, and our utmost care.

The next circle of people includes our extended families, co-workers, casual friends, and customers. We don't have as much emotional capital and time to invest in them, but if we're not careful, we can allow them to absorb too much of us, leaving us empty for the people in the center.

On the outside are people we pass each day at work and on the street. They have few claims on our attention. That doesn't mean they aren't important; it just means we recognize that we only have a given amount of time and love to offer others, and we have decided to invest wisely. Occasionally, we reach out to those whom Jesus called "the least of these" (Matthew 25:40), that is, the disadvantaged and downcast, but it is those in our *inner* circle whom we take with us, to care for and provide an example for them to follow. As we intentionally make a difference in their lives, the ripple effect will probably touch those in the second circle and perhaps even the third. But if we are never specific and purposeful about whom we most want to inspire, time will fly by, and we will have little positive impact.

The Bottom Line

Corporate executives are always mindful of the bottom line, which consists of both tangibles and intangibles. With regard to inspiration, the most significant entry on the intangible side is the spirit of the employees. It has a direct bearing on the tangible assets. If you don't believe it, consider this: many of the companies on Fortune's list of "100 Best Places to Work in America" are also some of the best performers on the stock markets. And though this is not a book about business growth, there is a direct correlation between a company's inspiration factor and its market value. Not only do inspiring organizations make more money, but they also have better employee retention and higher degrees of customer loyalty than their competitors. Similarly, parents who inspire their children not only enjoy deep and meaningful relationships with them, but also build value into their lives — increasing their kids' "bottom line."

In their insightful book, *The Value Profit Chain*, James Heskett, Earl Sasser, and Leonard Schlesinger define the "Profit Chain Proposition" as People, Service, and Profit. That doesn't mean profits aren't important, but profits come more readily when inspired, confident, competent, enthusiastic employees connect with one another in a desire to create inspiring experiences for their customers. Companies that operate by the Profit Chain Proposition are some of the most profitable, and, I believe, the most inspiring brands in the world. Some of these companies are American Express, Banc One, Ritz-Carlton, and Chick-fil-A. Their managers produce a wealth of intangible capital because they have learned the art and science of inspiring their employees, who in turn inspire their customers. Sounds like they're using the seven principles — and they don't even know it!

> *And though this is not a book about business growth, there is a direct correlation between a company's inspiration factor and its market value. Not only do inspiring organizations make more money, but they also have better employee retention and higher degrees of customer loyalty than their competitors.*

FEATURES OF *THE INSPIRATION FACTOR*

I get far more out of reading a book if I'm given an opportunity to take some time to wrestle with the issues the author presents. Perhaps you're the same way. For that reason, at the end of each chapter, you'll find two special sections entitled "Think About It . . . " and "Going Deeper." The first of these consists of questions for you to reflect on; the second is composed of exercises for you to complete. Both sections are designed to (1) help you gain valuable insights into your unique abilities to inspire people and (2) aid you in using your skills to have an even greater impact. These sections can also be used to stimulate rich discussions with your coworkers, family, and friends, or in a class or group. I hope you enjoy them.

MY PROMISE TO YOU

Many of us have attended management seminars until our derrieres ache. We come back, take a step or two to implement the techniques we learned — but little happens. What, you are probably asking, will be different about the information in this book? Great question.

The principles we'll explore in *The Inspiration Factor* focus more on character than technique. When we learn to be true to ourselves — take off our masks and become authentic — then we will care enough about people to uncover their dreams and value their abilities so that they are intrinsically motivated. In a nutshell, we'll focus more on right priorities, less on the bottom line.

> *The principles, stories, techniques, and tools in this book are designed to equip you to raise the inspiration factor in the lives of others.*

The principles, stories, techniques, and tools in this book are designed to equip you to raise the inspiration factor in the lives of others. Applying these principles takes some intention and effort, but they have a multiplied, powerfully positive impact on the people around us, on us, and on everything we touch together. And here's my promise to you: If you practice even one of the seven principles in this book, it will move the needle forward in your ability to inspire others. Use all seven, and you will change the very culture in which you live and work. Innovation will replace inactivity; sluggishness will transform into service. And the very atmosphere will change from one of self-interest into one bursting with cooperation. What could be better than that?

Think About It . . .

1. Who is the one person who has inspired you the most? What specific things did he or she do to raise the inspiration factor in your life? What impact has this person made on you?

2. Name someone you know who qualifies as a person full of "windspiration." How would you describe that individual? What impact did (or does) he or she have on you?

3. What do you want to get out of reading this book and applying the principles? Be specific.

Going Deeper

1. Make a list of the five to ten most enjoyable, successful periods of your life, and next to each, write the age you were at the time. Now make a list of the most distressing, boring, or discouraging times in your life, and again, put the age you were at the time.

2. Make a list of the people who inspired you most, and then make a list of those who drained inspiration from your life.

3. Draw a horizontal timeline on the page, beginning with your high school years and ending today. Now record on this timeline each of the successful periods and discouraging periods. Finally, add to your timeline the names of those who inspired you and those who drained inspiration.

4. Look at the timeline carefully, and describe the correlation between your level of inspiration and the people in your life. As you look at the charts, what conclusions do you draw about the impact of these people on your life?

5. Make a list of people who are in the center of your life today. What kind of impact are you having on them? What impact do you want to have?

6. Think about your customers, clients, donors, and children. How would you rate your inspiration factor in these relationships on a scale of 0 (nonexistent) to 10 (off the charts)? Explain your answer.

1   BE AUTHENTIC

"Authenticity means transparency, freedom from pretense.
The ego is terrified of authenticity." — *Andrew Cohen*

People can tell. We might be able to fool them for a while, but sooner or later, they know if we're real or not—and their perception of our authenticity defines our relationships with them.

For many years, I've been a fan of Dale Carnegie and his teaching about influencing the people around us. Though their focus at Dale Carnegie Training is on developing strong leaders for business, I have learned a lot that can be applied to all relationships.

A few months ago, I attended a Carnegie seminar with about thirty people, half of whom were from our company. As an exercise to show us the importance of connecting with people on an emotional level, each of us was asked to write out a "defining moment" in our lives and then stand up and share it with the group. It was fascinating! As we listened to each other's stories, I realized that we all fell into one of two distinct categories: those who were willing and able to share the painful problems we had experienced and the lessons we had learned, and those who couldn't or wouldn't.

Some participants told stories of failed marriages, bankruptcy, illness, prodigal children, and other gut-wrenching difficulties. They opened the door to a room in their hearts (that, for some, had been closed for a long time), and the whole group connected with them. As their stories progressed, each person shared how he or she had mustered the courage to take steps forward and find hope for the future. Each step brought new insights, and for many, the most painful moment in their lives ultimately proved to be a turning point toward more hope, love, and joy than they'd ever experienced. As they talked, the rest of us felt their pain and marveled at the courage it had required to turn calamity into progress. When they sat down, people reached out to pat them on the hand or shoulder. It was wonderful.

But a few people kept the door closed. They weren't willing to be vulnerable with us, and from their expressions, it appeared that they weren't willing to be honest with themselves. They knew they had to say something, but they settled for bland, superficial statements.

Stories of pain and courage break down walls of suspicion and build bridges of respect and trust.

One man talked about getting a speeding ticket, and the lesson he learned was to get a radar detector for his car. A woman tried to talk about a strained relationship with her sister, but her explanation was so full of excuses and obfuscations that none of us could follow the trail of her thoughts—and we were convinced that she couldn't either. In the end, she hadn't learned any lessons at all, because she hadn't been honest with herself about the pain she had experienced.

In contrast with our rapt attention to those who were authentic, listeners shifted in their seats, looked down instead of at the speaker, and coughed at odd times when those who were emotionally disconnected spoke. Even after these speakers sat down, the room was filled with tension.

Our experience at the seminar that day showed me more clearly than ever that those who are authentic about their pains and joys connect with people on an emotional level and have the greatest opportunity to inspire them. They have proven that even the most devastating problems in life don't have to crush us: they can make us stronger. Their stories of pain and courage break down walls of suspicion and build bridges of respect and trust. And their authenticity provides a safe haven for others, inviting them to uncover their own fears and dreams.

So, What's Your Story?

People who have gone through life's gristmill and found hope on the other side don't flippantly say, "I turned my scars into stars," or "I changed my importunities into opportunities." (This kind of language makes me cringe.) Superficial platitudes diminish the pain, the agonizing process of growth, and the courage required to overcome difficulties. *Real,* hard-won triumph over indisputable adversity results in positive and *profound* stories, never superficial ones. And these should be told with sincerity, not triviality.

Don't get me wrong. I'm not recommending that we bare our deepest, darkest secrets to everyone we know. Some people have earned our trust; we can be more vulnerable with them, but we are foolish to expose our hearts to untrustworthy people. So, start wherever you are. Find one person you trust, and take one step toward opening a door in your life that has remained closed for a while. Begin there, and see what happens.

It's All about Trust

Pulitzer Prize–winning political columnist David Broder once observed, "Authenticity means comfort in one's own skin, a minimum of pretense or artificiality, and especially consistency and predictability on matters of principle."[1] When I meet someone who's comfortable in his own skin, it's very attractive to me. When I go to a meeting, a convention, or even a dinner of hundreds of people, I can usually pick out such folks instantly. Actually, if you know what to look for, you can find them fairly easily. They are the ones who aren't trying to impress anybody. The look on their faces and their conversations tell you that they accept themselves for who they are. They know very well that they have flaws, but they also know their strengths, and they value them. Because they accept themselves, they can look beyond themselves to genuinely care about *other* people. And they do. These people ask great questions, and they really listen when people respond. That's attractive in any setting! Further, when they speak, they do so without ostentation. There's no *need* to put on airs. They know who they are, and they have no problem being authentic about it.

Authenticity is the foundation for building trust in any relationship — at work, at home, in the neighborhood, on the team, and everywhere else we go. Tragically, many of us spend an incredible amount of emotional energy and time trying to be someone we're not. We wear masks to project an impressive image — or to hide a fragile psyche. Wearing a mask, though, is surprisingly hard work. In fact, it's exhausting! We're always on alert, at all times looking for the right people to impress and the right thing to say to them. Our adrenaline level is sky-high because we're afraid we'll say or do the wrong thing. Then, when we do, we relive those actions and conversations, condemning ourselves for the dumb things we've said or done. That's not the way to live. As Peruvian author Carlos Castaneda said, "We either make ourselves miserable, or we make ourselves strong. The amount of work is the same."[2] Why not work toward being authentic?

Now, all of us want to put our best foot forward. That's not what I'm talking about. I'm talking about wearing a *mask*. Why do we do it? Because at the core, I think many of our lives are dominated by fear. I should know. I wore a mask myself for a long time. Our "masks" — psychological ones — go on when we feel insecure and want to make up for it. We may project enormous confidence, but behind the facade, we are afraid of being exposed as failures, ostracized by those whose opinions we value, or, in a word, *rejected*. So the masks go up, and with them we try to convince others that we're smart, witty, cool, or classy. These masks really aren't much different, then, from our old Halloween masks, the ones we wore as children. They accomplish the same exact things: changing the world's perception of us, while hiding who we *really* are. And worse, many of us have worn one so long that we have no idea what it's like to be authentic and to live without the mask. Our words, clothes, cars, gestures, hobbies—everything about us—are all designed to win approval, gain acceptance, and even to *control*. Why? Because, sadly, in some organizations, masks are valued more than authenticity, and those who project a particular image get the job and the promotions. So on goes the mask. And we think it's working, but in reality, we're driving people away, because they sense that we don't care enough about them to be authentic. In a phrase, they can see right through us—and it's anything but inspiring.

Who comes to mind as you read about wearing masks? Can you think of people who wear them? Are they good leaders? Do they inspire you? I doubt it. But they're everywhere to be found, and they try to fool almost everybody around them.

Masks can, in fact, effectively fool others—for a short time—but sooner or later, if we keep those masks tenaciously plastered to our skins, people realize they aren't getting the real thing from us. Then the problem isn't just the mask; it's the cold, calculated fabrication behind it. People will no longer trust us. They won't accept our attempts to motivate and inspire them. And they certainly won't let us into their lives, because we haven't let them into ours.

To be authentic, though, doesn't mean that we have to expose all the refuse of our lives for others to see. Yes, we must let others in if we hope to inspire them, but we must also be discerning when determining how much to share, when to share it, and with whom we share it. Just as people distrust those who wear masks, so also they distrust those who delight in describing their pain—in great detail and frequency. This comes across often as just an attempt to get others to feel sorry for the speaker. That's hardly a recipe for inspiration. But when people are straightforward and authentic in their sharing of their difficult experiences, making sure to top off their stories of hardship with the crowning ingredient—the *lessons learned*—they become heroes who can genuinely inspire others.

I think of a young woman who was in an abusive relationship in high school. We'll call her Nicole. The young man Nicole loved had beaten and intimidated her to the point that she had lost all confidence in herself. After a while, she deferred to him in every decision, even what and when she ate. She was emotionally crushed, only a shell of the vibrant young woman her family and friends had known.

On the day of her graduation, Nicole told her parents and siblings that she was pregnant. Aware of her boyfriend's abuse, they insisted that Nicole never see him again. She was too emotionally dependent on him to leave. But after several months of her parents' pleading, she finally came to a point of decision. Her parents had talked to friends across the country who were willing to let her raise her baby in their home. They had found a job for her too. The choice was excruciating for all of them, but she promised she would go.

Just hours before the flight was to leave, she was about to back out. Finally, a good friend offered to go along, and together, they got on the plane and headed west.

Over the next year, the fog in Nicole's mind began to lift. For a while, she hung on to the possibility of being reunited with her boyfriend. She heard rumors that he had a new girlfriend, and that she, too, was pregnant. But old dreams die hard, and she still hoped he would take her back. As time passed, though, hope turned into despair.

When the baby came, Nicole poured herself into her daughter. Gradually, her depression faded, and faint glimmers of hope began to reappear — and not hope for reconciliation with her boyfriend, either. Instead, she had hope for the *future* — hers and her child's. She worked and went to school to earn a degree. She developed a new set of friends, people who loved her but didn't try to control her. And as the years went by, she grew stronger and more resilient, with more hope for the future than she ever dreamed possible.

Today, her wisdom and love make her a magnet for other women in abusive relationships, and she helps them out of the wealth of her experience. Her story is a tragic one with a glorious ending, and she tells it authentically but also with discretion. In so doing, Nicole *inspires* everyone who knows her.

It would have been much easier for her to hide behind a mask. She could have chosen to live in shame and silence, keeping her story to herself. But authenticity pays great rewards. Perhaps the greatest reward will come in the future, when her daughter is grown and can genuinely grasp her mother's bravery. The sad story of a girl who made a bad decision to be involved in a relationship with an evil person will also be a story of a mother's undaunted courage to face reality, make hard choices, and carve out a new, hopeful, productive life for herself and her child. Already, this young lady inspires people, but her impact will only grow as time goes on—because she took her mask off.

What about you? Have you taken off your mask, or are you still wearing one? "What do I mean?" you ask. Well, for example, have you ever been in a place of leadership—but felt totally inadequate? It is at precisely those times that you may be tempted to wear a mask. Why? To project strength that isn't there, to protect yourself from exposure, to keep your feelings—maybe even your inadequacies—hidden. You feel incompetent, threatened, vulnerable—but believe it or not, these can become your finest moments of inspiration! This is when you need to muster the courage to remove your mask and honestly say to those who look to you, *"I need you."* That's authenticity: admitting that you need your team and that you can't make it through this time without them. Now, watch their response. The vast majority of people react very positively to such authenticity. It's the seed of trust that can grow and blossom into strong, effective relationships. It's also the seed of inspiration. Working for a man or woman who is unafraid to admit to occasional

That's authenticity: admitting that you need your team and that you can't make it through this time without them.

fear and weakness will cause others to be able to admit the same. Soon *everyone's* masks come off, and it is at this point that teams can really begin to work together, with their guards down and their cooperation up! That's the inspiration factor at work!

But to be the most effective that you can be at inspiring others, it pays to know what type of leader you are . . .

KNOW YOURSELF, BE YOURSELF: FOUR INSPIRING PERSONALITIES

Many of us labor under the misconception that we have to have a Tony Robbins personality in order to inspire people, but that's simply not the case. God has made *all* of us with a unique blend of personality, talents, gifts, and other strengths, and with them, we can inspire others. And the more we discover and live by our own God-given blends, the more fulfilled, effective, and inspirational we'll be.

For centuries, philosophers have recognized four distinct personality types. The ancient Greeks believed these emanated from four body fluids. Recent (and decidedly more scientific) personality theories also describe personalities under stress and in relationship to other types. For our purposes, we will identify four inspiring personalities as the *Commander,* the *Coach,* the *Innovator,* and the *Accountability Partner.* Let's examine these one by one.

The Commander

This person inspires others by his boldness, confidence, and determination to succeed. Commanders are motivated by challenges—the bigger the better—and they marshal every resource to accomplish their lofty goals. They cast a bold vision, and they make decisions quickly. Above all, they value action, not just words and emotions. Examples of Commanders include some of history's great military leaders, such as General George Patton and Napoleon. Unfortunately, under stress, such bold and determined Commanders become so fixed on their goals that they forget that people have feelings. They are impatient and demanding, determined to press ahead at any cost. At their best, Commanders accomplish incredible feats by marshalling resources and challenging people to excel. But at their worst, they try to control people by intimidating them. Threats become their primary motivational tool, and those closest to them begin to despise them. I've known Commanders who inspired their people by their clear, forward vision and their example of humility and brilliance, but I've also known men and women who, when the chips were down and their organization's future was on the line, yelled, cursed, and blamed everybody else for any perceived failure.

If you are a Commander, you are probably an outstanding leader when things are going well—communicating vision, organizing people, and setting an example of courageous, effective action. In times of stress, though, you run the risk of using people (instead of leading them) to get what you demand from them. What you need to remember, even in the good times, is that the Coaches and Innovators in your midst need more affirmation than you normally give, and your Accountability Partners require more explanations of the reasons behind your decisions. To inspire them, slow down a little, ask a few questions, and value their responses. Let the team come up with suggestions instead of bulling ahead with your own decisions.

The Coach

Coaches are personable, enthusiastic, and persuasive people who thrive on using their personality/persuasion to influence others. Their greatest strength is their ability to notice what people do well, sincerely affirm them, and put them in a position to succeed. In fact, when everyone on the team is succeeding, Coaches are at their best. They care about their team members, so they are most fulfilled when everyone is encouraged—especially when the people above and below appreciate them for it.

On the negative side, Coaches sometimes become enamored with the sound of their own voices and talk too much. And under stress, their thinking can become disjointed, and they may lose focus. In fact, Coaches can be

Their greatest strength is their ability to notice what people do well, sincerely affirm them, and put them in a position to succeed.

surprisingly fragile and feel easily hurt. When this happens, they become defiant and demand that others take sides—for them or against them. I've known athletic coaches, corporate executives, and other leaders who loved to build people into a cohesive unit to fulfill a high purpose. That's what Coaches do. But I've also known a few who, under pressure, lost their way, became distant, and blamed others for their own mistakes.

If you are a Coach, people love to be on your team because they know you genuinely care about them as individuals and will do anything to help them excel. But remember that Commanders will be frustrated if you talk too much without giving clear direction and letting them take action. Innovators and Accountability Partners need to be able to ask questions and get real answers, not just your "happy talk."

During times of stress, avoid labeling people as pro (all for you) or con (all against you), and avoid the extremes of blind optimism and bleak despair. In difficult times, ask questions—and *listen* to the responses. Value the varied contributions of each individual on the team. Provide clear direction for the Commanders and Accountability Partners (more than just a "pep talk), and give individual attention to questions from Innovators.

The Innovator

These people are sensitive, creative, and reflective. They value loyalty in relationships, so they make a few really close friendships. They are inspired by opportunities to be thoughtful and original in planning. And they ask a lot of questions, not because they want to challenge authority, but because they sincerely want to know the whys of every decision. Trust and the freedom to be imaginative are two premier values for Innovators.

Innovators thrive on new ideas and creative approaches—things that drive some of the other personality types crazy! Further, they inspire others to contribute their innovative ideas for problem solving. Steve Jobs is an outstanding example of how an Innovator can turn a company around with creative ideas and a can-do spirit.

The best teachers are probably Innovators who patiently instruct and inspire their students.

In the business world, Innovators form strong relationships and often see potential in people that others have missed. I've seen Innovators have a profoundly positive impact on people who felt lost or overlooked by others. Their sensitivity, though, has a dark side.

Innovators can crater under pressure, becoming discouraged and indecisive. Then, confused and seemingly lost, they revert to their analytical world instead of staying engaged in solving the problem. Even in the good times, they need a lot of individualized attention. But under stress, they need even more, when less is usually provided. And though change is the very lifeblood of Commanders and Coaches, Innovators typically view change as a threat and need plenty of time to respond to it.

If you are an Innovator, people trust you because you are loyal, sincere, and patient with them. You naturally provide nurture, but not much challenge. Yet remember that Commanders thrive on risk and action (the opposite of your profile). Accountability Partners appreciate your thoroughness, but they don't want to go too deep in the relationship. Learn to value their devotion to precision, but don't expect much of an emotional connection with them. And as for Coaches, they just want clear direction to make their optimism and energy effective. Make sure to give it to them.

In stressful times, Innovator, *be careful.* You can easily be run over, because you tend to become negative, overly sensitive, and hesitant to make decisions until you have all the answers. Muster the courage to step back into the fray and move forward, even if you feel somewhat uncomfortable with the level of risk.

The Accountability Partner

Accountability Partners are inspired by opportunities to concentrate on and follow *prescribed* systems to obtain *measurable* results. They lead best in organizations that value precision and tight controls. Because they are so detailed and disciplined, they consistently turn in excellent work even on the most mundane assignments, especially thriving in stress-free environments where expectations are clear and deadlines are firm.

Accountability Partners can become top executives in highly analytical or technology-related companies, but they play important roles in any organization. Their discipline and thoroughness give them the ability to help people do what they've already committed to do by asking questions and checking schedules. In other words, they inspire others to be more disciplined in order to be more *effective*.

Under stress, though, Accountability Partners tend to isolate themselves—especially from angry or out-of-control people—and revert to systems they can control. They feel very uncomfortable with risk and change of any kind. Their commitment is to the *details*, and this commitment on their part can make them appear harsh and judgmental, especially when they feel pressure to make others toe the line.

If you are an Accountability Partner, people value you because you are so devoted to excellence, but they may not understand what makes you tick. In good times, your clarity of expectations gives everybody tracks to run on. Be sure, though, to value the entrepreneurial spirit of Commanders and Coaches. They don't care as much about systems as you do, but they are willing to take risks that keep the organization moving. Innovators value reflection and detail, as you do, but they care more about feelings. Inquire about their personal lives, and then listen. In times of unusual difficulties, when you are tempted to hide from people and find security in the systems you know so well, remember that people need you. Get out there, interact with them, ask questions, affirm them for trying to find answers, and give them pats on the back for each step toward success. You have the ability to help people stay focused even in the middle of chaos, but to play that role, you have to stay engaged and not retreat.

THE WHOLE TEAM

Some of us have a clearly identifiable personality type, but many of us are a combination. At the end of the chapter and online, you'll find an inventory to help you identify your profile. Your scores will show you whether your profile consists of one or more than one type. As you analyze your scores, keep in mind factors such as your stress responses and where you are in the organizational hierarchy. Many of us respond differently under stress than we do normally, and some of us relate up the ladder in a very different way than we relate to peers or those who report to us, so keep these things in mind.

WARNING!

A word of warning: far too often, we value only the Commanders and Coaches as inspiring personalities, because they are most verbal and visible. What's worse, these strong personality types often pigeonhole the Innovators and Accountability Partners as "too analytical" or "too negative"; meanwhile, they themselves are often the most inauthentic people in the organization, ensuring their failure at inspiring *anyone*. My point is, *every* person can play a valuable role in inspiring others — *whatever* your personality type. Begin by discovering who you are.

Take some time — right now — to go online (www.inspirationblvd. com) and take the Personality Profile to identify your personality type so that you can learn your strengths and weaknesses, be comfortable in your own skin — and be *authentic*. Authenticity requires both a dose of knowledge and a measure of courage. The inventory will give you some insight, but it's up to you to have the courage to yank off your mask. But if you will do it, people will trust you, and you will have taken the first step toward *inspiring* people.

THINK ABOUT IT . . .

1. Without writing down any names, identify a few people who wear clearly identifiable masks. How would you describe these masks? How do they project an image? What might they be trying to hide or protect?

2. What are some ways that wearing masks prevents authenticity? What is the effect on the person wearing one? What is the effect on relationships with others?

3. Which of the four inspiring personality types seems to fit you?

4. How does identifying their personality type help people take off any mask they may be wearing and become more authentic? How would it help you?

GOING DEEPER

Go online and take the inventory on the four inspiring personality types. A sample is included here.

Inspiration Blvd. Personality Profile

Introduction

This inventory contains 20 statements. Don't think too long or too hard about your answers. Indicate the answer that best fits your experiences. In some cases, two answers may seem equally true of you, but pick one. You'll probably find that you are a blend of a couple of the major profiles. The statements address your motivations, needs, and desires in relationships; stress responses; leadership goals; and communication style. After you complete the scoring sheet, read the descriptions of the four profiles: Commander, Coach, Innovator, and Accountability Partner; and answer the questions under "Review and Application" at the end of the scoring.

Circle the letter to indicate the response that best fits you.

1. I am most energized by:
   A. Discovering new ways to help people and achieve success
   B. Challenges
   C. Motivating others to succeed
   D. Systems and numbers that actually work

2. When tasks are given to me, I:
   A. Get going immediately
   B. Find the best system to do the job
   C. Think about the best and most creative way to accomplish the job
   D. Get others involved and discuss each person's role

3. To be most effective, I need:
   A. Individual attention and affirmation
   B. A creative, stress-free environment

C. Plenty of authority and high goals
D. Specific directions and control over the process

4. When I'm in a group, I:
   A. Am often very quiet
   B. Delight in meaningful conversations with a few people
   C. Enjoy telling and hearing great stories
   D. Am usually the center of attention

5. When I feel stressed, I:
   A. Become demanding and impatient
   B. Withdraw and focus on what I can control myself
   C. Get my feelings hurt and become confused and hesitant
   D. Feel hurt and become defiant

6. I work best in an environment that:
   A. Is friendly but has clear direction and expectations
   B. Gives me plenty of opportunity to take charge and generate action
   C. Allows me to influence others and build a team
   D. Provides plenty of time to think, plan, and discuss options

7. I feel most fulfilled when:
   A. A lot of people appreciate the impact I've had on them
   B. Others appreciate the new ideas I've offered
   C. I have accomplished goals nobody thought I could achieve
   D. I've checked off all the boxes on my list

8. When a new idea is communicated:
   A. I need to know how it impacts what I'm already doing
   B. I'm ready to make it happen
   C. I carefully think about it to see if it makes sense and can be improved
   D. I feel thrilled if it was my idea and discouraged if it wasn't

9. When people ask for my opinion:
   A. I'm absolutely sure I'm right
   B. I ask a question to clarify it
   C. I give it, often without thinking before I speak
   D. I let others answer while I analyze the question and consider my response

10. The influence I want to have on others is to:
    A. Encourage them to find new, creative ways to succeed
    B. Provide accurate data in a timely manner for them
    C. Challenge their socks off
    D. Motivate them to succeed individually and as a team

11. People see me as:
    A. Disciplined, consistent, and efficient, but sometimes aloof
    B. Warm, fun, and verbal, but sometimes off track
    C. Kind, reflective, and patient, but sometimes fragile
    D. Direct, intense, and driven, but sometimes impatient

12. When people who report to me struggle or fail, I:
    A. Kick them in the butt to get them back on track
    B. Try to help them understand what went wrong so they can make adjustments
    C. Become their best cheerleader
    D. Do it myself next time

13. To help others make decisions, I:
    A. Provide plenty of accurate information for them
    B. Ask questions to help them discover the best path
    C. Make the decision for them if they take too long
    D. Encourage them to do what I think they should do

14. When people who report to me succeed, I:
    A. Throw a party!
    B. Give them even bigger challenges as a reward

C. Offer heartfelt congratulations
D. Am happy for them, but to be honest, I wonder how they did it, because they didn't seem to know what they were doing

15. The kind of direction I give is:
    A. Clear, quick, and practical
    B. Personal and encouraging
    C. Precise with deadlines
    D. Thoughtful, patient, and open to discussing options

16. When people are unresponsive to my leadership, I often:
    A. Feel hurt and confront the person personally
    B. Feel tense and go back to what I can control
    C. Feel confused and analyze the situation
    D. Feel angry and demand a response

17. I feel like quitting when:
    A. Nobody appreciates me
    B. I feel pressure to make snap decisions and do meaningless tasks
    C. Hell freezes over (I can always figure out a solution)
    D. Expectations aren't clear and deadlines aren't enforced

18. My verbal skills are:
    A. Controlled and cautious
    B. Strong and direct
    C. Positive and personal
    D. Warm, relaxed, and interactive

19. When I think I'm being treated unfairly, I:
    A. Insist that systems and rules be followed
    B. Enlist others to be on my side
    C. Feel very discouraged and hopeless
    D. Become furious and impatient

20. The people I've led for an extended time would say I'm:
    A. A bold visionary
    B. A great friend
    C. Very dependable
    D. Their greatest fan

Scoring

Circle the responses you indicated for each statement, and add the total in each column.

	Commander	Coach	Innovator	Accountability Partner
1.	B	C	A	D
2.	B	C	A	D
3.	B	C	A	D
4.	B	C	A	D
5.	B	C	A	D
6.	B	C	A	D
7.	B	C	A	D
8.	B	C	A	D
9.	B	C	A	D
10.	B	C	A	D
11.	B	C	A	D
12.	B	C	A	D
13.	B	C	A	D
14.	B	C	A	D
15.	B	C	A	D
16.	B	C	A	D
17.	B	C	A	D
18.	B	C	A	D
19.	B	C	A	D
20.	B	C	A	D
	_____	_____	_____	_____

Review

If one of the totals has a score of 12 or more, you have a fairly clear inspiration personality profile. And if two of them have a combined score of 15 or more, but neither is over 10, you are a strong blend of these two.

Reflection and Application

1. Which profile (or combination) best describes you?

2. What are your strengths in motivating others?

3. How have you seen those strengths affect people around you?

4. Who are the specific people in your family, your company or organization, or your church that you want to inspire?

5. How do you normally relate to all four types of people?
   — Commanders

   — Coaches

   — Innovators

   — Accountability Partners

6. Consider the descriptions of each type of person. In good times, what are some ways you can inspire each one more effectively?
   — Commanders

   — Coaches

— Innovators

— Accountability Partners

7. In stressful times, what do you need to do to overcome your natural tendencies so you can motivate each kind of person instead of using them or annoying them?
   — Commanders

   — Coaches

   — Innovators

   — Accountability Partners

8. What is one thing you will do today (or tomorrow) to motivate a particular person more effectively?

2 CONNECT WITH OTHERS' DREAMS

"Run your fingers through my soul. For once, just once,
feel exactly what I feel, believe what I believe, perceive as I
perceive; look, experience, examine, and for once, just once,
understand." – Anonymous

A young man—we'll call him Rick—graduated from a prestigious university with a degree in marketing, and soon landed a job with an ad agency in Denver. For the first few months he would describe his position as "a dream come true," because he got to work on national accounts with his colleagues, and he felt he was making a significant contribution. As Rick became more comfortable in his role creating ad campaigns and designing the ads, the owner of the company praised him to employees and clients. Still, at every meeting and in every way, the owner himself found a way to become the center of attention. Rick thought this behavior was normal for someone who had taken the risk to start a company.

A few months into Rick's employment, a crucial deadline for the company's major client approached, and the owner's demeanor changed drastically. He was no longer the lighthearted, creative leader Rick knew him to be. He turned into a bear. In meetings with the creative team, the owner blurted out idea after idea without asking for or accepting input from the rest of the team. Rick tried to offer his opinion a couple of times, but the owner blew him off and chastised him for being "so negative."

The atmosphere of the entire company changed during those intense weeks. Everyone tiptoed around the owner in fear of getting chewed out, and seldom did anybody offer an opinion on anything. It was like a big, awkward dance, with every person moving in tandem with the owner's mood. Creative people, though, can't stand it when they aren't allowed to express their ideas, so several team members tried again and again to offer suggestions. (They knew better than to tell the boss that his ideas were bogus.) Still, the owner didn't listen to anyone about anything. The whole world, it seemed, revolved around "the boss."

One day, a lady who had been at the company a year longer than Rick offered a creative concept in a meeting, but the owner again ignored her. After the meeting, she came up with a strategy that might work. She wrote down her idea and put it on his desk. A few days later, he bounded into the conference room to announce his "bold, new, innovative idea." It was hers, but he didn't give her any credit at all. He claimed it was his brainstorm.

This experience taught Rick that the company's actual mission was very clear and very limited: to make the owner a hero at all cost. After the first few thrilling weeks on the job, he gradually realized that his contributions would never be valued, and he dared not ever express his dreams. They didn't matter to his boss at all.

NOTICE, NAME, AND NURTURE

We all have dreams and desires. They may be big or little, outward or inward, clear or cloudy, but unless we are severely wounded emotionally and are hiding in a shell of self-protection, we all have aspirations. One of the most significant insights of my life is that I, as a manager, can tap into my employees' dreams and reap rich benefits for them, for me, and for the company. A company's overall success, after all, can be highly compatible with each person's cherished desires—enough so that everyone feels fulfilled. Of course, not every person's dream is for the company to succeed, but most—especially those whose own needs are being met—*will* achieve personal satisfaction from the company's success. Why? I believe that God has put it in the hearts of all people to live for something *bigger than themselves.*

At the same time, though, most folks enter their professional field with the hope that their career within a successful company will help them

A company's overall success, after all, can be highly compatible with each person's cherished desires — enough so that everyone feels fulfilled.

achieve *their own* life's dreams as well. One of the greatest joys of my life, therefore, is uncovering others' dreams and providing resources to fulfill them. I'm sure you feel the same. To do that, you and need to *notice, name,* and *nurture* their dreams.

We *notice* others' dreams when we watch their faces and listen to their voices to see what thrills or impassions them. Some of our dreams are self-focused: to own a second home in the mountains, to tour Europe every year, or to have enough money for a comfortable retirement. Another layer of our dreams, though, connects our skills with our hearts. We may want to be a public speaker and shape others' lives, or lead a group of people who want to grow richer and stronger in some way. But many times, our dreams are shaped by a need we feel called to meet. We may want to pour our resources into an orphanage, build low-cost homes, or care for the elderly.

If we ask a few questions, we can often quickly discover what makes people tick. I ask questions such as:

— "What attracted you to the company?"
— "What activities energize you and feed your soul?"
— "What keeps you up at night, either from worry or excitement?"
— "Where do you think you can have the greatest impact?"
— "Do you feel more comfortable with relationships, facts and figures, or managing processes effectively?"
— "If you could write a slogan for your life, what would it be?"
— "What makes you cry, and what makes you laugh?"

Many employees think that the only thing their managers care about is their performance and their contribution to the bottom line. Sadly, they're often right. But if we ask questions such as these, we will uncover real dreams — and a person's dreams are the source of his inspiration.

As I've talked to hundreds of men and women over the years about their dreams, I've discovered that putting a *name* to these dreams makes an enormous difference. I listen intently as they answer my questions, and then I might say something to summarize their response, such as:

- "You never give up. You're a true *competitor*."
- "You have an intuitive ability to sense what people are thinking and feeling. You're a real *mind reader!*"
- "You are so persuasive — but without being pushy. I've never seen a better *influencer*."
- "You have an uncanny ability to assimilate an enormous amount of information — and still figure out what's really going on. You must be a *genius.*"
- "You can get a team to work together incredibly well. I think you'd make a great *leader.*"

Observing people's strengths and naming their dreams often leads to additional questions, such as: "Have you thought about being the CEO of your own company? What would that feel like?" or "What resources or experiences do you need to maximize your abilities and fulfill your dreams?" Quite often, the act of naming their dreams crystallizes people's thoughts and gives them a handle on the future they've never had before. Your involvement is a tremendous gift to them. You may be the first person (at least in a long time) who has investigated, uncovered, and invested in their dreams.

Noticing and naming are important, but the third ingredient is crucial too. When people have trusted us enough to share their dreams, we need to *nurture* them and provide resources and advice to help fulfill them. In the vast majority of cases, people were attracted to their current roles because they consciously or unconsciously saw their jobs as channels of opportunity to fulfill their dreams. For that reason, it's usually not difficult to help people see how their daily responsibilities could be stepping-stones to those goals. A major reassessment of a person's job description may be required, but it's worth it, because aligning an employee's personal dreams with the company's goals makes for a powerful combination. It unleashes amazing energy and creativity in that individual. On the other hand, when personal goals and company goals *cannot* be aligned, every activity seems forced.

> *Every person has dreams; it's our privilege to help each one identify them, and then find ways to align them with the company's goals so that both company and employee can be productive.*

Last year, Debbi and I had a wonderful vacation in the French Alps. To get from place to place, we rented a small, fuel-efficient car. Unfortunately, while the car was great on gas, it struggled to make it up the steep mountain roads. The Lamborghinis and Ferraris that passed us from time to time *flew* by as if we were standing still. The way I felt in that little underpowered car is the same way unaligned employees probably feel all day every day. It's demoralizing—but it doesn't have to stay that way. Every person has dreams; it's our privilege to help each one identify them, and then find ways to align them with the company's goals so that both company *and* employee can be productive.

Having said that, how do you even begin to align an employee's dreams with the objectives of the corporation? Considering the person's best interests is a good starting point. Leaders should make every effort to see to it that what's *best for the employee* is high-priority, even in the midst of pursuing the company's goals. This commitment from leaders optimizes employee performance, reaping outstanding results, and smoothing any necessary transitions. If you are a leader, look aggressively for opportunities to develop, train, and expose your people to others who can help them reach their dreams. That's nurture.

For the past twenty years, I've followed this process of noticing, naming, and nurturing the dreams of people who report to me, and almost without fail, it has changed the atmosphere of the office. When people are convinced that we genuinely care about the deepest desires of their hearts, they become more enthusiastic, creative, disciplined, committed, and flexible than ever before. I know. I've seen it over and over again. But when we fail to connect with their dreams, the air turns cloudy (if not poisonous), energy evaporates, and suspicions multiply. People feel used instead of valued, and they are easily distracted by anything and everything.

WHY DON'T WE CONNECT?

The diagnosis is easy, but the treatment is difficult. The primary reason we, as managers, parents, and other leaders, don't connect with people is stress. We don't pay attention to the desires, needs, and dreams of others because we're too hurried and harried—i.e., too "stressed"—to think about anyone else.

Actually, stress isn't the problem—it's *excessive* stress. In his book, *Margin: Restoring Emotional, Physical, Financial and Time Reserves to Our Overloaded Lives,* physician Richard Swenson observes that moderate levels of stress bring out the best in people. Appropriate challenges stimulate creativity and inspire people to accomplish higher goals. Like the proverbial "frog in the kettle," however, our stress levels can rise so gradually that we don't even notice. As tension slowly rises, we experience detrimental effects of *too much* pressure. When excessive levels of stress feel normal, we fail to notice the problem, and then, of course, we fail to make changes. Under intense pressure, every aspect of our lives is affected: our abilities aren't as sharp, we make bad decisions, patience evaporates, and consequently, we experience even more stress. In many cases, we even experience physiological symptoms, such as headaches and stomach problems; our most important relationships suffer; and we become gradually less and less effective, eventually leading to discouragement, depression and burnout.[1] In other words, our focus soon becomes *our* health, *our* emotions, and so on. It should come as no surprise, then, that the greater the stress, the higher the self-preoccupation—and the lower the inspiration factor.

The pace of life today is far faster than that experienced in earlier generations. We demand quick solutions instead of expecting change to take seasons and involve long processes. We have redefined "normal" as swift, complete resolution to life's problems, and we are annoyed with anything less. And with RAZrs, BlackBerrys, and iPhones in hand, we expect to get more done in less time, and we rush from one thing to another, trying to make a busy life into a full life. Amazingly, though technology has promised to give us more free time, we actually live at a more frantic pace with less time for reflection, leisure, and relationships. It's no wonder we're stressed.

In his article, "Diagnosing Hurry Sickness," in *Leadership* magazine, popular author John Ortberg identified two signs of stress: speeding up and multitasking.

> **Speeding up.** You are haunted by the fear that you don't have enough time to do what needs to be done. You try to read faster, lead board meetings more efficiently, write [plans] on the fly, and [in conversations] you nod more often to encourage [people] to accelerate. . . .
> **Multi-tasking.** You find yourself doing or thinking more than one thing at a time. . . . The car is a favorite place for this. Hurry-sick [leaders] may drive, eat, drink coffee, listen to [CDs], shave or apply make-up, direct . . . business on the car phone—all at the same time. Or they may try to watch TV, read *Leadership*, eat dinner, and carry on a phone conversation simultaneously.[2]

In short, hurry-sick leaders are in a world of their own. But to inspire other people to greatness, we have to get beyond our own world and reach into theirs, connecting with their dreams. We *can't* connect with them, though, while we're rushing past them to get more stuff done. We have to change our values, define the

We have to change our values, define the difference between the "important but not necessarily urgent" and the "urgent but not important,"3 and focus on the truly important things in life — the people around us.

difference between the "important but not necessarily urgent" and the "urgent but not important,"[3] and focus on the *truly* important things in life — the people around us.

A friend of mine told me about a pediatrician who cared for his children years ago. This man was an eminent doctor, on several boards, and at one time the president of the American Pediatric Association. Few professions are more demanding than being a doctor, and this man's schedule was packed beyond belief. My friend told me, though, that when this doctor walked into the examining room, "he acted like there was no other child in all of God's creation — only mine. He gave my daughter complete, focused attention, and he patiently answered every question we had. And in fact, he took time to give my wife a recipe for dressing at Thanksgiving. I don't know if I've ever felt as cared for in all my life."

Another example of carving out care in a busy world is my wife, Debbi. As president of Grizzard Communication Group, she has enormous responsibilities, but when anyone walks into her office, she has the amazing capacity to close out all the noise of her phone, BlackBerry, to-do list, and memories of things she needs to do but still hasn't done. She focuses instead on the person sitting in the chair across from her. Debbi is all there, and the listener knows it. And whatever the hope or complaint expressed, together they find a solution that both meets the client's goals and fulfills the employee's aspirations.

When we make people a priority, we take time to notice more than the obvious traits that everyone sees. For example, I used to introduce my team members at presentations by listing their titles and accomplishments, but as I've become more observant, I now introduce them by describing the impact of their talents and identifying their aspirations. This subtle shift changes everything. My team members feel understood and valued, and our clients realize that we practice what we preach about making people a priority. It raises the inspiration factor for every person in the room.

When Debbi and I went to Europe, we traveled to Florence and saw some work by the Renaissance master Leonardo DaVinci. I was intrigued by this enigmatic genius, so I bought a biography to read on the flight home. The book described his artistic achievements, but it also explained his incredible gift of observation. He sometimes watched birds for hours, noticing every conceivable nuance of their wings and flight. He wrote volumes of notes (strangely, in minute script and in a reverse mirror image) and made countless drawings of the human figure, landscapes, and even inventions— often centuries ahead of their time. His genius could only be captured and expressed because he took plenty of time to observe his surroundings and catalog his observations. In the same way, we will only become outstanding, inspiring leaders if we stop racing from one thing to another and stop long enough to observe the habits, dreams, and abilities of those around us.

We will only become outstanding, inspiring leaders if we stop racing from one thing to another and stop long enough to observe the habits, dreams, and abilities of those around us.

CONNECTING WITH THE DREADED "ANNUAL REVIEW"

Many of us, managers and employees alike, dread annual reviews because we perceive them as disruptive, negative, or shallow. Let me offer a different approach: Ask the employee to identify at least three personal dreams and connect those with corporate goals. The discussion, then, can focus on clarifying the person's dreams and the specific ways the company can become a vehicle to fulfill his greatest desires. Your role will be to provide training and other resources so that the company's objectives become a platform for the employee's passion, skills, and energy. You can imagine the enthusiasm this discussion will generate!

Each of the seven principles in this book offers a choice: to keep going the way we've been going, with the same, predictable results; or to change. As long as we let stress steal our time, drain our energies, and erode our passions, we'll continue to miss golden opportunities to notice, name, and nurture others' dreams. If, however, we intentionally carve out space in our lives to live for the things that are truly important instead of being harassed by the urgent, we'll have plenty to give to others. Change, though, requires insight, commitment, and courage, but insight comes first—and we only gain insight into people by taking time to notice, name, and nurture their dreams. Is it worth it? You have to decide for yourself. From my experience, I think it is. My wife, interns, employees, children, and friends would say so too.

How to Connect with Others' Dreams

Tom Harrison is the Chairman and CEO of Diversified Agency Services (DAS), which manages Omnicom Group's holdings in a variety of marketing disciplines serving national and international clients through more than 700 offices in 71 countries. Tom is an innovative leader whose passion is to inspire an entrepreneurial spirit in his staff and his clients. To make sure the CEOs of the 160 DAS companies feel challenged and motivated, he hosts three biannual gatherings, called Jazz Meetings, so they can come together, hear a great speaker, discuss an important topic, and learn creative ways to serve their employees and clients more effectively. He also launched a blog to help the Omnicom family tap into the entrepreneurial DNA of clients. As every top manager knows, there's an inherent risk in stirring up innovative, aggressive staff: Some of them may start competing companies. But this possibility doesn't bother

An environment that encourages creativity and risk-taking will attract and keep outstanding men and women.

Tom. He believes that an environment that encourages creativity and risk-taking will attract and keep outstanding men and women. And he's right. Executives at Omnicom are convinced that Tom cares passionately about them, their individual dreams, and their shared dreams.

You may not be at the top of the corporate ladder, like Tom, but you can still connect with others' dreams, even at the lowest management level. Let me offer a few specific suggestions to help you identify people's dreams and provide resources to fulfill them.

1. Help them craft a personal vision statement.

Notice that I didn't say, "Tell them to write a vision statement." Far too frequently, when people are told to write a "vision statement," they come up with something that isn't compelling and fails to capture their hearts. Crafting a personal vision statement is a process that shouldn't be rushed. For it to be effective as a life marker, it has to reflect the person's genuine desires, ones that may be hidden behind his own masks and the expectations of others. The questions designed to uncover a person's dreams are a good place to start, but don't stop coaching people until they have something that makes their eyes light up and their hearts sing. It's work, but it's worth it—for both of you.

One of the best resources for writing a personal vision statement is *The Path* by Laurie Beth Jones. Jones instructs people to begin by listing words that describe their abilities and character, not just their titles or roles. For some, this activity is a struggle at first, but soon they realize that they are far more than salespersons, administrators, managers, or consultants. They are, instead, *caring, dedicated, loyal, trustworthy, helpful, kind,* or *visionary.* As these words are used to craft a personal vision, a powerful new sense of direction begins to unfold. (Go to inspirationblvd.com for an exhaustive list of descriptive words.)

2. Create an environment where it's safe to take risks . . . and fail.

Some people, like Commanders and Coaches, love risks. They thrive on competition and challenges—the bigger the better. Most folks however, see risks as threats instead of opportunities. Our job is to help them face their fears and overcome them so that risks actually become opportunities for growth.

When my daughter Brittany began to play tennis, she was afraid of hitting the ball out or into the net. Like the vast majority of beginners, she tentatively hit the ball in a soft loop to maximize the possibility that it would go in. I knew that it would take her a long time with this approach to develop the skills and confidence she needed to excel at the game. "Brittany," I told her, "don't worry about hitting the ball out or into the net. You can hit it out, or you can hit it into the net, but hit it hard! Just don't hit it like a sissy."

She hit it hard. In fact, she smoked the ball on every shot! Soon she began to learn how to control her stroke, so more and more shots were good. Before long, teammates, coaches, and parents were amazed that she hit the ball so powerfully and accurately. Now she hits the ball harder than anyone I've ever played. But she could never have done it had she continued to allow her fears of making mistakes dominate her game. To succeed, she first needed permission to fail. And when I gave it, Brittany experienced freedom to learn and grow.

The same principle works in every job and every relationship. Mark Twain said, "Twenty years from now you will be more disappointed by the things you didn't do than by the ones you did do. So throw off the bowlines. Sail away from the safe harbor. Catch the trade winds in your sails. Explore. Dream. Discover." Many people fail to pursue their dreams because they feel caught in a web of fears—the fear of failure, rejection, being

> *Leaders who genuinely inspire others do so by tapping into their dreams, eliciting the best from them, and ultimately changing their lives.*

exposed, looking silly, and others. When we give such people a safe place to take risks without condemnation for failure, many people respond like a bullet shot from a gun. They take off! Some, though, aren't sure we really mean it. They're afraid we'll criticize them or correct them (or even terminate them) if they fail. Reflective, suspicious people need more time to be convinced that we mean what we say, and often, they need to see us give others freedom to fail before they'll take risks themselves.

A few people have an inherently negative attitude about their jobs. To them, work is supposed to be boring, demanding, and difficult. Failure, they believe, is an institutional and personal norm, and the concept of aligning their personal dreams with the company's objectives isn't even on the radar screen. These people need a radical reorientation of the meaning of work. For them (and for everyone on your team) I suggest you take time at an upcoming staff meeting to stake out a new direction. First, write your company's objective on a whiteboard or poster and explain, "This is where the company is going. Any questions?" Then give each person a piece of paper and ask each to describe the kind of reputation he or she wants among other employees, management, and clients or customers. Give the group a few minutes to complete this task. Then ask them to connect the dots: write a list of the specific activities they can perform that will achieve the corporate goals and enhance their reputations. After they've written their responses, provide plenty of time for people to share their answers, and sincerely encourage them for their insights. Tell them you want to meet with them individually to fine-tune their plans. Then, in the weeks that follow, meet with each person to affirm him, adjust his job description if necessary, and set new expectations. This process can reenergize every person in your office and foster a willingness to step out and attempt bold ventures without fear of censure.

3. *Provide regular, specific affirmations.*

Many managers and parents make one of two common mistakes (or maybe both): (1) they make the colossally inaccurate assumption that if people are doing well, they don't need affirmation, or (2) when they do affirm, they use global, nonspecific language. Neither inspires anyone. And know this: Whether your job is managing or parenting, *everyone* around you is thirsty for affirmation. In fact, some of those who seem to want it least actually need it most. A wise person once said, "People live for encouragement, and they die without it." Every person, even those who seem to be rock-solid islands of stability, needs others to notice and celebrate what they do well.

> *People live for encouragement, and they die without it." Every person, even those who seem to be rock-solid islands of stability, needs others to notice and celebrate what they do well.*

Sandy is a young lady who works for a nonprofit organization, and everybody marvels at her skills and temperament. One day, her CEO told me, "Sandy's an exemplary employee. If I could craft someone using someone else's DNA, that person would be just like Sandy. She is bright, kind, creative, punctual, and a great team player."

"Have you told her that?" I asked him.

"At her last review," he replied.

"When was that?"

"Six months ago."

I pressed a little. "I'm quite sure she'd like to hear you say that she's a valuable person on your team. You may not know it, but some other companies have heavily recruited her. She chooses to stay because she is committed to the mission here."

He thought for a moment and then said, "No. I don't think she cares what I think about her. She's strong. She doesn't need that kind of coddling."

But dreams die for lack of nurture. On the other hand, regular, specific affirmations are the sunlight, water, and fertilizer of people's dreams. To be meaningful, though, they have to be specific.

Telling someone, "You're great!" doesn't mean very much at work, at home, or in volunteer organizations. Become a student of the people who report to you, and verbalize the positive things you see. (If each person takes the Inspiration Blvd. Personality Profile and you can identify each person, you'll have a lot of specific information to work with.)

When we fail to affirm people, we unwittingly create an environment where suspicion and distractions grow. People want to know where they stand with their manager. When they hear nothing at all, or only hear corrective words, doubts and insecurity begin to form. In this atmosphere, people become easily distracted from the task at hand, preoccupied instead with self-protection. They start spending time imagining what might be going on that they don't know about or thinking about finding another job. Teams, like all relationships, don't remain static: they are ever in the process of growing stronger or weaker, building or eroding trust. To keep them strong, *every team member* needs affirmation.

This principle also applies to a nonprofit organization's relationship with its donors. If leaders affirm that donors' dollars are making a specific difference in people's lives, the donors feel engaged and energized – and they want to continue to be a part of the vision. Conversely, according to Grizzard's research, many donors stop giving precisely because they don't feel appreciated by the organization. Affirming donors, then, is an essential ingredient in the plan to fulfill the nonprofit's vision, because the mission of the organization becomes the donor's mission too.

Similarly, when employees are affirmed, the company's mission also becomes the employee's mission. There is a direct correlation between affirmation and loyalty. In fact, show me a leader who is slow to affirm, and I'll show you a group of employees with wandering eyes and hearts.

4. Observe people's positive emotional responses.

Some of us are astute in noticing the negative responses we see in others, but we need to be just as aware of their positive responses.

Obviously, when we see someone's eyes light up and she gets excited, it is evidence of a desire being fulfilled (or at least addressed). But enthusiasm isn't the only positive response to watch for. When people are gripped with the dream of making a difference, they are passionate about those they want to help. Passion may surface as joyful exuberance; it may also appear as a "holy disgust." Many leaders observe that real change often comes only when people become truly disgusted with the status quo. Something, they determine, simply *has* to change. Their attitudes are similar to that of Popeye, who, when reaching the tipping point of exasperation, growls, "That's all I can stand, I can't stands no more!"

Many leaders observe that real change often comes only when people become truly disgusted with the status quo.

When you see enthusiasm in someone, don't take it for granted. Explore it, ask questions, and pursue the underlying motivations. And when you see holy disgust, don't be alarmed. Anger at injustice and tears of compassion are good and right. In fact, they are obligatory for a healthy person with a dream to make a difference.

5. Be a resource to help people reach their dreams.

Your words of affirmation are vital, but words aren't enough. Your commitment to people—and your ability to truly inspire them—is demonstrated when you take *action* to help them progress toward their dreams. It's really not that hard. A young man told me his dream was to learn to be a public speaker, so one day at lunch we went to the bookstore and I bought him a CD of great speeches. He was blown away. A few minutes and a few dollars convinced him that I was under the rock with him, and our relationship rose to a new level that day. Another time, I was on the receiving end, when my good friend Laurie Beth Jones was a valuable resource for me. One day I mentioned to her my passion for studying the great speeches of the twentieth century because I wanted to be a more effective communicator. The next week she sent me a beautiful book containing fifty of the greatest speeches of the last one hundred years. I appreciated her kindness even more than the book itself.

Valuable resources are readily at hand. HR departments can help managers identify courses, seminars, coaching, degree programs, and countless other opportunities to help employees reach for their highest goals. Too often, though, these resources remain underutilized simply because managers fail to ask about them.

6. Celebrate every step forward.

Great managers make a big deal out of people's progress, and they are creative in their celebrations. It doesn't have to be expensive to be meaningful. You can throw a party at the finest resort, or you can call your team together and give them a handmade plaque to commemorate their accomplishments. And celebration doesn't have to be limited to things that happen in the company. You can just as easily memorialize a person's accomplishments *outside* the office walls. One district manager of a large company even appointed one of his staff as the unofficial Director of Ambiance. This person's job is to keep celebrations and affirmations high on the priority list and make sure they are meaningful. You should do the same. Remember, people are trying to reach their dreams. Each step toward those dreams is one step less that they have to take. Celebrate!

THE RISK OF DILUTION AND THE POWER OF ALIGNMENT

Over the years, as I've talked to executives about these principles, most of them intuitively grasp how they can inspire their people more effectively. Yet for a few, the attitude seems to be, "Who's got time for all this inspiration stuff? We've got jobs to do." And, true, inspiration does take time. So does connecting with other people's dreams. *Too much* focus on individuals' dreams can dilute the energy and take attention away from the corporate vision.

But I've seldom seen this problem occur. More often, I've seen corporate and nonprofit executives wringing their hands because their people aren't motivated sufficiently. They've tried a myriad of techniques, carrots, and sticks, but little has changed.

Yet when we tap into people's dreams and show them how the corporate vision can be a vehicle to help them reach their goals, we experience the incredible power of alignment. It's a beautiful thing to see, and often it happens almost spontaneously. Time after time as I've watched people uncover their dreams, they've become more committed to the company than ever. More than that, their trust grows in the manager who cared enough to talk to them about what matters most to them. I've seen good employees become great, and those who had been labeled as "problems" become effective, pleasant members of the team.

I've seen good employees become great, and those who had been labeled as "problems" become effective, pleasant members of the team.

Is it important for managers to learn to align the company vision with each person's dream? Yes. In fact, I believe it has a multiplied impact. The ability (or inability) of managers to inspire their people shows up in tangible ways, such as higher or lower profits, and in intangible ways, like the way employees connect with customers because they feel believed in and supported. And it makes a difference in employee retention. People send résumés to a company because of the company's brand and reputation, but they usually leave because they can't stand their supervisor. Employees deeply appreciate supervisors who genuinely care about their dreams and support their efforts to reach them.

For years, I've started team meetings by asking people to share what positive traits they've noticed in each other. At first, people talked about task-related things they'd seen, such as, "Penny, you stayed late to finish that report," or "Your presentation was excellent, John. You were really well prepared." These comments were very encouraging, but in a month or two, people began to notice and name character qualities, not just performance: "Susan, you showed a lot of courage when you handled that client," or "I couldn't believe how patient you were, Phil, when that guy kept asking the same questions!" As people felt more understood and affirmed, they were more open to sharing their dreams with the rest of us. Gradually, everyone realized that we valued more than each person's performance; we valued one another. As I reflect on a particular team that gelled especially well, I realize that we had at least one of each of the personality types in our group, and they noticed different abilities and strengths in each other.

Valuing people beyond their performance is especially important in families. When we look beyond our spouse's and children's mistakes, encourage them to take risks even if they fail, and help them pursue their dreams, they flourish. Robert Lewis, author of several books on leadership and men's development, observes that there are three statements every child needs to hear often: "I love you"; "I'm proud of you"; and "You're good at [a skill, talent, or activity]."[4] These statements, when spoken from the heart, give a child (or a spouse) a strong foundation for pursuing his dreams for the future. The same is true in the marketplace.

Inspired employees make life much more enjoyable for their managers. Team members accomplish more, so Commanders are happy. They work together more effectively, so Coaches feel fulfilled. When they feel free to try new things and make mistakes without being condemned, they become more creative under the leadership of Innovators. And inspired employees aren't as resistant to following rules and using systems, so Accountability Partners can sleep well at night. When employees' dreams are noticed, named, and nurtured, everybody wins. Start doing it today. It's a choice that only you can make.

"I have learned, that if one advances confidently in the direction of his dreams, and endeavors to live the life he has imagined, he will meet with a success unexpected in common hours." – Henry David Thoreau

THINK ABOUT IT . . .

1. On a scale of 0 (totally relaxed) to 10 (in a knot), rate your stress levels over the past few months. What are some of the causes of your stress? (Stress can be caused by positive changes, such as weddings and promotions, as well as negative ones, such as debt and disease.)

2. How have you tried to resolve each stressor? Have you instead tried to escape from it or ignore it? Explain your answer.

3. How does stress affect your ability to manage, your energy, and your capacity to interact with others to uncover their dreams?

4. How has stress affected your pursuit of your dreams?

GOING DEEPER

Use these questions with at least two people on your team. Find a time when you aren't buried under deadlines, or if that's a consistent problem, carve out uninterrupted time to ask the questions.

Prepare for each interview by writing down at least two specific strengths you see in the person, and if possible, identifying the times and topics that have evoked positive emotions.

1. Begin by explaining that you want to get to know each person on the team more fully, and you want to ask some questions about what matters most to them.

2. As you ask these questions, listen intently, and ask follow-up questions. If the person says something significant, you can say, "Tell me more about that." You might ask, "What happened next?" or "How did that affect you?" Don't rush through the questions. It's better to have a rich discussion about one or two than to try to cover all of them. The questions are:

   - What attracted you to the company?

   - What do you like to do in your spare time?

   - As you think back over your life, what are the things (not necessarily business related) that have given you the most fulfillment?

   - What events, relationships, needs, and challenges of the past year have generated the most passion in you? Explain what happened and how you responded.

   - How would you describe how you want your life to count? What kind of impact do you want to have?

   - What are some resources the company and I can provide to help you have that kind of impact?

3.   When you've finished asking the questions or feel you've asked enough to have a valuable discussion, summarize by repeating what you heard the person say. Make this statement in terms of the person's dreams: "From what you said, it seems that your life's dream is to . . ."

4.   Then ask, "What are some ways I can help you take steps toward your dream?" Listen carefully. People may not believe you really want to help, or they may not have any clue about steps they need to take, so they certainly can't explain how you can help. Don't push this offer, but tell the person that you'll be looking for ways to help in the future. Thank him or her for the time, and end the interview.

5.   Within a few days of the interview, take the initiative to mention the person's dream again, but not in a public way that might cause embarrassment. If, however, you interview everybody on your team (which I highly recommend), you might ask people to share their dreams in a team meeting if they feel comfortable talking about them. Mutual understanding and support can work wonders to build trust and cooperation!

6.   At least on a monthly basis, talk to each employee about his or her dreams, and ask what you can do to help. Find resources and look for alignment within the company so that the company's goals become stepping-stones for the person's growth.

3 SEE IN OTHERS THE ABILITIES THEY DON'T SEE IN THEMSELVES

"Finding the right work is like discovering your own soul in the world." – Thomas Moore, Irish poet, singer, songwriter

A person's dreams and strengths are inextricably linked, but they aren't the same thing. One is about the heart; the other is about the hands. Dreams tap into people's deepest desires and strongest motivations, but they can wither and die without nurture. We must help the people we lead to maximize their abilities. Only then will they feel enthused about what they do every day.

When I was in junior high school, I already had a glimmer of a vision for my future. I wanted my life to make a difference, and I believed that my future would involve communicating verbally and in writing. At the end of that year, my English teacher announced to the class, "If any of you would like to take a creative writing class, let me know." I jumped at the chance. Raising my hand, I told him that I wanted to sign up. He frowned and said, "I don't think that's a good idea for you, Terry. You struggle too much with your writing now. There's *no way* you can make it in that class." I was crushed, but I trusted him to know what was true about me. He saw no potential, so I concluded there must not be any. I'm sure he had no idea how his words discouraged me.

In stark contrast, that same year my history teacher saw more potential in me than I saw in myself. I wasn't a very good student, and though he and I hit it off well in class, I didn't make stellar grades in history (or any other class, for that matter). At the end of the first term, he sat at his desk, looking at the honor roll. After a few minutes, he looked up and said, "Mr. Barber, I don't see your name on the honor roll. I certainly thought you'd be on it."

"Me?" I replied incredulously. Nobody had ever told me he expected me to be an honor student.

"Of course," he replied with calm assurance. "You're bright, you grasp concepts very well, you're curious, and you have what it takes to be a very fine student." He smiled and nodded toward me, "I expect to see your name on the list in the future."

Until that day, I had made Bs and Cs in every class, but from that moment on, I never made anything less than an A in history. I only wish all my teachers had seen potential in me, as my history teacher did.

THE POWER TO BUILD OR DESTROY

As managers, leaders, teachers, and parents, we have the amazing power to build or destroy, to be a launching pad for success or to crush people under the weight of discouragement. Our ability to recognize others' abilities makes an enormous difference in their motivation, their confidence, and the course of their lives. In that brief window of time in junior high, two teachers had a profound impact on me. In those classes, I was the same person with the same ego, the same intellect, and the same desires. But one saw potential; the other saw impossibility.

Leaders who genuinely inspire others do so by tapping into their dreams, eliciting the best from them, and ultimately changing their lives.

One gave me confidence to excel in history and take honors classes the rest of my academic career, and the other filled me with doubt about my abilities and myself. Today, I still enjoy the benefits of one man's belief in me, and though I've learned a lot about writing and communicating since that devastating day in English class, I sometimes still suffer nagging doubts about my ability to communicate with others.

WHEN THEY NEED IT MOST

Overcoming ingrained negative messages is a lifelong chore, one that requires persistence, courage, and the support of at least one person who believes in us. Some never make it. But I'll give you an example of one who overcame.

William Manchester's two-volume biography of Winston Churchill, *The Last Lion*, chronicles the life of the man who was considered "the greatest man of the 20th century."[1] Churchill's life, though, was a checkerboard of fantastic successes and colossal failures. His father, Lord Randolph Churchill, sent him off to boarding school and wrote his son scathing letters describing his disappointment in him. His socialite mother neglected him because she was preoccupied with her many lovers, including the duke of Windsor. In his early life, the only person who genuinely cared for Winston was his nanny.

In the army, young Winston was determined to prove himself, both as a soldier and as a correspondent in India and in the Boer War in South Africa. Soon, though, the lure of politics led him to run for Parliament, and he was elected as one of its youngest members. He rose quickly in power and popularity and served as Lord of the Admiralty during World War I. Soon, though, he was blamed for the disastrous strategy of invading Turkey, and he resigned his post to return to the infantry and the trenches in France.

After the war, Churchill's star again began to rise, and he became Chancellor of the Exchequer, only one step away from being prime minister. However, in the crisis over Irish independence, he resigned his role in the government and became a lowly "backbencher" in Parliament. Everyone said that his career was over. He had come close to being prime minister, but now he suffered from what one member of Parliament said was "a zigzag streak of lightning in the brain" — a statement that acknowledged his brilliance but also his unpredictability.

When Adolf Hitler became chancellor of Germany in 1933, Churchill instantly saw the threat and began to expose Hitler's menacing power. His opposition to Hitler, though, wasn't shared with many others in government. They saw Hitler as a potential ally against the Soviet Union, not a probable threat to England. Churchill led a small handful of men who refused to believe Hitler's repeated assurances that Germany wanted peace. As Hitler began taking territories in central Europe, Churchill founded and led a growing movement called "Arms and the Covenant" to rearm England for the war he was certain soon approached. Gradually, sentiment in Parliament and in the nation began to move to Churchill's side, and momentum to oppose Hitler rose to encouraging levels.

Then, in 1936, Edward VIII abdicated his throne for the love of his life, Mrs. Simpson. The nation was outraged that he would defect from his God-given responsibilities as the nation's sovereign to marry an American divorcee. Churchill, always loyal to the monarchy, spoke in Parliament to defend his friend the king, but he severely misjudged the mood of the nation. Parliament revolted against him, shouting him down when he tried to continue his speech. Public ridicule of the rearmament movement's leader resulted in the collapse of "Arms and the Covenant" and the reversal of fortunes for his political enemies in Parliament, who believed money spent on arms was a greater threat to England than Hitler's Wehrmacht. Now, the appeasers were again respected and trusted. Of them Churchill lamented, "There is no plan of any kind for anything. It is no good. They walk in a fog. Everything is very, very black."[2]

Churchill returned home in disgrace. He had known failure before, but nothing like this. He was now isolated and scorned more than at any time in his up-and-down career. For days, he sat silently in his chair. His depression hung over him like a storm cloud. In his own account of the years leading up to World War II, Churchill recalled this dark moment and commented, "All the forces I had gathered together on 'Arms and the Covenant' were estranged or dissolved, and I was myself so smitten in public opinion that it was the almost universal view that my political life was at last ended."[3] Few in the nation realized that crushing debts he had accumulated by lavish spending, in spite of his meager salary, compounded his despair. He wrote books and articles to earn extra money, but they weren't enough. He was broke and broken.

Churchill's life is a study in the power of negative messages, not only to wounded people, but also, perhaps, to inspire them to prove themselves in spite of others' opinions.

Though no one recognized it at the time, this moment proved to be pivotal in the history of Western civilization. As a desperate act in his bleakest moment, Churchill contacted his friend, American industrialist and financier Bernard Baruch, to ask him to help find him a job in the business world. Politics and writing simply hadn't worked for him. Perhaps he could play out the last years of his life by earning a good salary in a major company.

Into Churchill's psychological and political abyss stepped five people who continued to believe in him. Baruch gently brushed aside Churchill's request and encouraged him to remain in politics. Three men in Parliament remained loyal, and Clemmie, Churchill's wife, was steadfastly dedicated to her brilliant husband. Their faith made all the difference — for Churchill, for England, and for the West. Encouraged by their belief that his consummate abilities would be used to the fullest in coming years, Churchill remained in Parliament. Four tumultuous years later, Churchill became prime minister and led England through what he called "our finest hour" of defying Hitler alone and remaining free until America entered the war to turn the tide in World War II.

Churchill's life is a study in the power of negative messages, not only to wounded people, but also, perhaps, to inspire them to prove themselves in spite of others' opinions. For Churchill, the negative messages spurred him to action, for a time. But sooner or later, the ability to stand alone to overcome negative messages fades and fails. He almost left the political arena. Had it not been for the support of a *few* who recognized in him what he could not see himself, the benefits of Churchill's leadership would have been lost to the *many*. In people's darkest moments, they need someone to step into their lives, recognize their strengths and abilities, and give them hope for the future.

FOCUS ON THE POSITIVE

Many studies show that our self-perception is shaped to a significant degree in childhood by the messages communicated to us. Psychologist and author Sarah Radcliffe asks parents these practical questions: "Do you offer a steady stream of compliments, praise, and unconditional positive regard? Or is it, 'Hurry up! You're going to be late! Put that down before you break it! Clean up that mess right now! Eat your breakfast. Brush your teeth. Make your bed. The bus is coming. Leave your brother alone. Where's your homework?'" Radcliffe recommends that parents give at least four positive messages (words, hugs, etc.) for every corrective one.[4] For many of us, however, the negative far exceeded the positive. It wasn't that our parents didn't love us; they just didn't know how to communicate it. Even when the number of positive and negative messages are equal (or weighted toward the positive), sensitive people dwell on the negative ones they've heard. These messages cut like a knife, leaving them bleeding and wounded. As adults, they may receive many affirmations for their performance, but their minds remain haunted by statements such as:

- "You'll never amount to anything."
- "You're stupid."
- "Why can't you do anything right?"
- "I can't believe you messed it up again!"
- "You're a failure, and you'll always be a failure."

What do we focus on in our communication with employees, interns, staff, spouses, and children? When a child comes home with three As, two Bs, and a D, what do we react to and talk about? The D! Certainly, some corrective action needs to be taken for the low performance there, but the impact of focusing on the negative is devastating. The child would be far more encouraged and motivated if the parent celebrated the three As first before addressing the D.

When we go over an employee's performance review, do we breeze through the eighteen positive parts because "she already knows that anyway" and spend 90 percent of the interview on the two areas that need improvement? That seems a bit out of balance.

Marcus Buckingham, coauthor of *Now, Discover Your Strengths* and author of *The One Thing You Need to Know*, cites a study by the prestigious Purnell School in Pottersville, New Jersey, which surveyed employees' perceptions. From 2005 to 2007, the respondents were asked about how much of each day they spent using their strengths. Over these three years, the answers slipped from a dismal 17 percent, to 14 percent, and finally to a tragic 12 percent. If managers want to motivate their staff by having them work in the areas of their greatest abilities and effectiveness, they clearly need to do a much better job.

In a talk given at the Willow Creek Summit in August 2007, Buckingham identified several common myths about managing people. One of these is: "You grow the most in the areas of greatest weakness." Not true, says Buckingham. Actually, people grow most in the areas where they are most confident and motivated: their strengths. When we focus our attention on their weaknesses, we stunt their growth and limit their potential.

Here's another myth: "A great team member puts his strength aside and does whatever it takes for the team to succeed." This sentiment sounds noble and is occasionally true, but if it becomes the norm, the team member's motivation declines, and the whole team suffers. A person who contributes most to his team exercises his strength the majority of the time. Team leaders, then, need to know the strengths of each person on the team—even if the member doesn't know them himself—and tailor assignments to fit as much as possible. The employees, in turn, will excel to a great extent by default. They're doing what they're good at, and when it earns them kudos, it will inspire them to do better still. And the gift goes on. Each new success will raise your staff's inspiration factor by degrees.

The principle of focusing on strengths instead of weaknesses is just as true in the family room as it is in the boardroom. Parents need to observe their children carefully to see how God has crafted them—with their unique blend of personality, gifts, and passions. King Solomon, one of the wisest leaders in history, wrote, "Train a child in the way he should go, and when he is old he will not turn from it" (Proverbs 22:6 NIV). Each child has a "way he should go" based on his character/skill set blend, and even children in the same family often differ markedly from one another.

I know a couple with three children. Two of the kids are very gifted athletes—the boy in football and baseball, and the girl in volleyball. Both received college scholarships. Their other son, though, is about as coordinated on the field or court as cooked spaghetti. Yet early on, these parents—also very athletic—recognized that he had an almost innate musical ability. To their credit, early in their musical son's life, they recognized and accepted the fact that he's different. They then poured as many hours and resources into his musical development as they did into the lives of their sports-loving kids, inspiring their young artiste to musical greatness. Today, he can play the piano beautifully. In some families a child who is different is often ridiculed and labeled a "loser," but in this one, they all celebrate each other's successes. More power to 'em!

Positive messages can have a phenomenal impact. My wife, Debbi, remembers a specific conversation with her grandfather that inspired her for life. When she was eleven years old, she sat with him on a woodpile outside his home near Rome, Georgia. He was whittling. As they were talking, he suddenly stopped and turned his gaze to her. Holding his carving knife, he looked into her eyes and said, "Debbi, you're going to make something of yourself. I know it!" At that moment, his words meant the world to Debbi, and she remembers his words and the look in his eyes even today. From that day forward, she has been strengthened by her grandfather's confidence in her. She told me, "If Grand-daddy thought I could be somebody, who was I to argue with him? Even today, when I give a presentation, his affirmation continues to inspire

> *Holding his carving knife, he looked into her eyes and said, "Debbi, you're going to make something of yourself. I know it*

me and give me confidence." And all because a Southern grandpa recognized a little girl's strengths, even when she could not.

A "360 PROFILE"

Before we can focus on others' strengths, we may need to begin with an analysis of how much we operate out of our *own* strengths. A number of self-tests and consultant-processed profiles are available to help people reflect on activities that have brought them success and fulfillment. Some of these go back to childhood; others center on more recent work experience. All of these, though, attempt to surface patterns of experiences in the past on which to build a plan for the future. A successful analysis will uncover one's primary areas of competence, interest, and fulfillment, and these should be reviewed in light of the person's personality profile.

One of the most helpful types of inventories is a "360 profile" that provides insight from many different sources. I recently had one administered for myself. A set of questions about me was sent to my boss, several peers, a couple of clients, my wife and children, and two friends. The input I received was fascinating, and in a few cases, very surprising. I received a lot of affirmation for my leadership and communication, but several people reported that I, like most men, sometimes fail to communicate as fully as I need to. In tension-filled situations, I become very reflective and quiet so I can carefully consider the alternatives and consequences of choices. The feedback from others in my 360 profile helped me realize that people were confused when I became quiet; they expect me to be outgoing and verbal all the time. The solution has been fairly simple. Now when I become pensive, I make sure to tell people that I'm not withdrawing from them and I'm not upset with them. I just need a little time to think. This single insight and adjustment has reduced confusion and raised the level of understanding. That's a very productive outcome.

The 360 profile offers input from multiple sources up, down, and across the organizational hierarchy and outside it. It promises to give the most accurate feedback on both your strengths and the areas that need improvement. A sample 360 profile is included for your use in this book.

OPENING OUR EYES

Why do so many leaders and managers fail to help others succeed? Because they make false assumptions. Let me illustrate.

With regard to budgeting, many companies and nonprofits use what is known as "institutional budgeting" in which they assume that, since this year's budget was just fine, they need only make minor adjustments for next year's budget to work equally well. In contrast, I recommend "zero-based budgeting," starting from the ground up each year to think through goals, which shape objectives, which inform strategies, which require budgetary allocations. This approach takes nothing for granted. It looks at the cold, hard facts, as well as opening eyes to greater opportunities. It shuns the status quo and concentrates on possibilities. It takes more effort, but it promises to be far more effective than institutional budgeting.

Unfortunately, many times we take the "institutional budgeting" approach with people. We make the assumption that they are doing just fine—but we're looking at them through the lenses of our own desires, needs, and goals. If they fit what we expect, we leave them alone to roll along again for another year . . . or another decade. Before long, we find that we, like Jim Collins's illustration of the bus in Good to Great, are riding along with the wrong people on the bus, or with people in the wrong seats because we haven't taken the time and trouble to find the best fit for them.

When we put a team together, we should begin with no assumptions. We can then take time to ask questions, uncover dreams, identify abilities, and help people become great. If we become leaders of an existing team, we may have a bit more work to do, because their culture has already been established to some degree. Still, a little time, a few great questions, and good listening will bring to the surface the goals and desires of each team member. Then we can make adjustments to their roles, so they are more motivated and effective. The same principles and processes apply if we are

We need to value them as people — not as cogs in the corporate machine — and align their abilities with the company's goals so that we can inspire them to excellence.

already leading a team. We can carve out time to dig deeper into team member's lives to find out what makes them tick. We need to value them as people — not as cogs in the corporate machine — and align their abilities with the company's goals so that we can inspire them to excellence.

As you learn more about each person's personality profile, you can tailor your affirmations and challenges for each one. The Commanders on the team don't care much about warm words, but they almost burst with excitement when you look at them and say, "Jim, we have a really tough job to do, and I believe you're just the guy to get it done. Are you up for it?" The same approach, however, might cause an Innovator to wilt. To that person, you might say, "Sarah, we've tried to fix this problem a number of ways, but we haven't been able to do it. Would you put a team together to come up with a creative way to solve it?" A Coach likes to lead a team, but she will be even more motivated if you explain how working together will accomplish two goals: solving the problem and building people.

The Accountability Partner isn't motivated by creativity, but if you explain how his role of producing and following a prescribed system will help accomplish the goal, he's all in. Your job is to identify the abilities in these people — they may not see them for themselves!

STOP WASTING TIME

It's vital to help people identify strengths, but some organizational consultants report that it's even more important to help them identify areas in which they *aren't* gifted. Too many people pursue the wrong career for years, and at the end, they've wasted a lot of valuable time. I worked with a young lady who wanted more than anything in the world to be head of human resources for her company someday. She took courses, attended seminars, spent time with HR department staff, and applied for every position that opened there. The problem was that she lacked perception about people. Inventories administered to her by the HR staff confirmed this time after time, but for four years, she refused to believe it. Finally, she bugged the staff so much that they set up a meeting for her with the HR director. He then told her, in no uncertain terms, that she wasn't cut out for the department. Finally, and very reluctantly, she shifted her focus back to what she was doing: accounting. It took her a while to adjust her expectations, but today she's thrilled to be where she is. "What in the world was I thinking?" she said to me. "I don't even pick up on cues from my best friends. Why would I think I'd be terrific in HR?"

I've seen other employees rivet their desires to being speakers, corporate trainers, or the top executive in the company. I'm always wary when someone is ambitious for *position* rather than *impact*. This may seem like too fine a distinction, but I don't think so. At some points in my career, I've thought ambition was a virtue; at other times, I've condemned it as a vice. Ultimately I've learned that ambition is neutral — it depends on the object of its desires.

When people tell me they want to move up to a top-level position or find a role that gives them a platform to be the center of attention, I ask a few more questions. I want to know if they really care about making a difference, or if they simply want the power and applause that the position promises. Power and applause—these two temptations can lead good people off track if they're not careful. There's nothing wrong with having powerful positions as long as we don't crave the power in order to dominate people. Similarly, there's nothing wrong with applause if it's a gift from those who appreciate our efforts. Our motivations, though, become skewed and self-absorbed if we live for positions and approval instead of for impacting people for *their* sake. And self-absorbed leaders fail convincingly at inspiring their staff. They're wasting their time. So, again, though it's important to help others see abilities in themselves that they may not see, it's just as important that we be real in the opposite sense. If employees clearly lack abilities that they are certain they possess, it's cowardly to let them continue to suffer under a delusion. It will only lead to profound failure.

AUTHENTIC THANKS

One of the most powerful but often most underutilized management tools is a simple "Thanks" to people who have done a good job. Whether you know it or not, a "Thanks" to someone who may not realize that he has a gift or talent can make the lights come on. It can mean the difference between recognizing his abilities and being inspired to use them and staying forever in the dark about what he's good at. A word of genuine appreciation can make a person's day (or week)—but it has to be authentic. Authentic gratitude is a sweet aroma, but if it seems forced and phony, it stinks.

A friend of mine, Will, told me that he used to work for a guy who thought he was God's gift to the business world. He always had the right answers and never made a mistake. You know the type. This guy demanded to be the center of attention, and he expected to be praised by everybody in the company. Not surprisingly, people despised him. He barked out directions all day, every day, and ridiculed his staff with sarcasm. As he cut them to ribbons, not only did he laugh, but he even expected those who weren't the target of the moment to laugh with him.

After Will had been on the job for a year, his boss, during a corporate meeting, got up to recognize Will's accomplishments. "As I sat there listening to him," Will told me, "I felt nauseated. I wanted to throw something at him. He said all the right words, but he sounded completely insincere — because he was insincere." Did Will's boss inspire him in any way? You tell me: Will transferred to another division a few weeks later.

We don't have to be great communicators to say, "Thank you." We just have to mean it. And we can be sure that every person in our world — those up the corporate ladder, down the ladder, peers, spouses, children, friends, strangers, and everybody else — will light up when we look him in the eye and say, "Thanks. I really appreciate what you did."

One of the trends among younger workers is a growing thirst for appreciation at work. Postmoderns love their freedom and independence, and they aren't attracted to long-term corporate commitments. For them, security comes through relationships, and appreciation seals and lubes those relationships better than anything else. Obviously, then, the more you know about a person's personality type, dreams, and abilities, the more accurately you can frame your words of praise and thanks.

Some time ago, I decided to be more intentional about thanking people and praising their efforts, and it's paid off big-time. To an analytical person on our team, I said, "Tammy, you did a great job breaking down this complex job into sequential steps so that all of us could understand the critical path and implement the plan." To Tim, our team's creative director, I said, "And you captured the concept beautifully in your design. Now everyone who sees the image instantly understands what we're trying to communicate." To another team member, I said, "Barbara, you did a fantastic job assessing the cost of the project in terms of human resources. Your contribution made a huge difference to our success." From the very first time I spoke to each one this way, the entire mood of our team was transformed. They took off in an incredibly positive direction. Soon, whenever we met, each individual instantly knew the scope and value of the contribution he or she would make, and collectively, they were highly motivated — that is, *inspired* — to excel even more.

GRATITUDE AND THE BOTTOM LINE

In *The Elements of Great Managing*, Rodd Wagner and James K. Harter researched the impact of employee recognition. The results were staggering. In companies ranging from health care to banking, when employees felt appreciated, they did better work and connected more effectively with clients and customers. The authors observed, "A large multi-company analysis puts the average benefit of such a shift of recognition at 6.5% greater productivity and 2% higher customer engagement . . . where each percentage point equates to hundreds of millions in sales for a Fortune 500 company."[5] Translation: *thanking employees for their good work makes a difference in the company's bottom line.*

My personality enables me to relate to people very easily, so for years, I didn't think I had to try too hard to show appreciation. I was wrong. Being thankful is so important that it deserves at least a few minutes of attention and planning — and we get better with practice. When I began to be more intentional about thanks by thinking for a few minutes before every team meeting, I began noticing more reasons to thank people. And the more I noticed, the more specific I could be. I never want to be phony. Like my friend, Will, I am disgusted by such charades. I want to notice what people have done to contribute to the success of the team and point it out as authentically as I can. It makes a difference — to them, to me, and to the effectiveness of our team.

> *I want to notice what people have done to contribute to the success of the team and point it out as authentically as I can. It makes a difference — to them, to me, and to the effectiveness of our team.*

To be effective in affirming the abilities of team members, a leader needs vision, insight, and the ability to value skills in others that are different from his own. He needs vision to see the whole picture: the corporate and project goals, the contribution of each team member, and how they can work together to be most effective. He needs insight into each individual to know how to fit his or her personality, motivations, and skills with the responsibilities. And he needs to be humble enough that he isn't threatened when others have certain talents that surpass his own. Good leaders may be able to perform all the tasks of every person on the team, but great team leaders develop and inspire people to become more skilled in their individual fields of expertise than he is.

When we recognize and affirm others' abilities, they feel empowered, and they take more initiative. Old fears fade, and hesitation evaporates. In their place comes the freedom to be themselves and contribute powerfully to the team. And as people enjoy using their strengths, managers spend less time trying to pump up their staff and more time on strategically guiding them to be more effective. It's a lot more fun to ride in a car with a powerful engine that's running on all cylinders than to have to push it uphill. Yet too many managers have been pushing their staff so long that they're all exhausted and resentful. It doesn't have to be that way. Every team member whose strengths are recognized, validated, and appreciated by the manager is far more likely to be a powerful piston in the machine. So be smart. Fill their tanks with praise.

Noticing, Naming, and Nurturing . . . Again

In Principle #2, we discussed the importance of noticing, naming, and nurturing others' dreams. But as you can see, it's equally important to take these *same* actions with regard to people's abilities. The spirit of an inspired team is your company's *most valuable* intangible asset, but it's an asset you will never own if you don't take the time to affirm your team members. *Notice* the abilities that they can't see in themselves; that's what this chapter is all about. *Name* them, both privately and in front of others. And *nurture* their skills so that every team member becomes an integral — and suc-cessful — part of a well-oiled machine. It's the only way to inspire.

Think About It . . .

1. What are some negative messages you heard as a child? as an adult? How have these affected you?

2. What one person has noticed and affirmed your abilities most powerfully? What has been the impact of that person on you?

3. Think about the people at work and at home. What are their strengths? (It might help to think in categories of tasks, relation-ships, analysis, and vision.)

4. Write out a sentence that you would like to say to each of them about their strengths.

5. Say it with authenticity as soon as you can.

GOING DEEPER

Use the 360 Profile on the next page for yourself and for the members of your team.

Inspiration Blvd. 360 Profile

This tool is designed to give people accurate and comprehensive feedback from those who know them best. Many managers use the 360 Profile to gather perceptions and offer insights to those who report to them, but individuals can also take the initiative to gather feedback from coworkers, family members, and friends.

If you are orchestrating the profile to get feedback on yourself, here's how it works:

1. Select someone—a professional coach, mentor, or supervisor— to help you choose the people who will be involved. Later, this person will also help you interpret and apply the results.

2. Go online to www.inspirationblvd.com to set up the 360 Profile. On the site, list the names of your coach (or supervisor, if that person is going to coordinate the profile for you) and the participants. Make sure to write down the password that people will use to fill out the inventory on you.

3. Ask the ten people you selected to take about 20 minutes to go online and fill out the inventory with you in mind. These ten people should include:
    - your direct supervisor or director
    - four peers
    - three family members
    - two friends

4. Instruct these people to go to www.inspirationblvd.com and click on "360 Profile." They will type in your name, their names, and the password, and then complete the inventory about you. Give them a deadline determined by you and your mentor, probably no longer than two weeks away. Explain that their answers will be compiled for a report and will be kept strictly confidential.

5. After a week, go online to see who has not yet completed the profile. Send a reminder to those participants.

6. When everyone has completed the profile, we will send a report to your coach or mentor.

7. Set aside at least two hours to go over the results.

If you are not a manager but are simply a team member, you can still use the 360 Profile. Simply follow the steps above for each team member, listing yourself as the coach and the direct supervisor.

This instrument contains three sections. As you complete each one, click "Next" to go to the next one.

For 1–20, use this scale:

5   Always
4   Often
4   Sometimes
2   Seldom
1   Never
0   N/A

Section 1

— Character Traits

1. Consistently honest and trustworthy
2. Accepts constructive criticism with poise
3. Has an infectious, optimistic attitude
4. Rigorously objective about opportunities and problems
5. Punctual and prompt to complete assignments

— Skills

6. Eager to learn new skills
7. Efficient and effective
8. Prioritizes responsibilities
9. Effective in leading others
10. Committed to excellence

— Teamwork

11. Works with others to find common ground to solve problems
12. Listens well and asks good questions
13. Has realistic expectations of self and others
14. Delegates with clear expectations
15. Gladly celebrates others' successes

— Resolving Conflict
    16. Responds to authority with appropriate respect
    17. Communicates clearly under stress
    18. In tense situations with others, first tries to understand the other person's point of view
    19. Anticipates problems before they arise
    20. Doesn't hold grudges or take revenge

Section 2

Rate each of these qualities on a scale of 0 (a big problem) to 10 (a great strength):

Loyal	0 1 2 3 4 5 6 7 8 9 10
Enthusiastic	0 1 2 3 4 5 6 7 8 9 10
Helps others uncover dreams and abilities	0 1 2 3 4 5 6 7 8 9 10
Visionary	0 1 2 3 4 5 6 7 8 9 10
Detailed	0 1 2 3 4 5 6 7 8 9 10
Trustworthy	0 1 2 3 4 5 6 7 8 9 10
Builds a team	0 1 2 3 4 5 6 7 8 9 10
Inspiring	0 1 2 3 4 5 6 7 8 9 10
Analytical	0 1 2 3 4 5 6 7 8 9 10
Tells great stories	0 1 2 3 4 5 6 7 8 9 10

Section 3

Answer each of the following questions as clearly and honestly as possible. The person will be given your answers in a report. Remember, your answers will be kept confidential. A report listing all of the responses for each question will be provided to the person being profiled. Please write one to four sentences for each question.

1. What exceptional character qualities, skills, and abilities have you seen in this person? (What traits can you easily notice, name, and affirm?)

2. In what relationships (at work or at home) does this person have the most positive influence? Explain your answer.

3. What are this person's passions? What causes his or her eyes to light up?

4. What relationships and recurring situations cause him or her to lose focus, energy, and enthusiasm?

5. What can you imagine might be this person's highest and best impact a year from now? Five years from now?

4 Speak with Credibility

"The most tragic thing in the world is a man of genius who is not a man of honor." — *George Bernard Shaw, Irish literary critic, playwright, and essayist*

In the fall of 1865, students at the struggling Washington College in Lexington, Virginia, watched their new president actively structure a new academic curriculum. But though his involvement with this endeavor was full-on, he moved very slowly around the campus, whether on his majestic gray horse, or on foot. He also looked very, very old. And yet . . . that man was perhaps the most highly respected person on both sides of the recently reunited nation.

Four and a half years earlier, Robert E. Lee had been a colonel in the United States Army. As Southern states seceded from the Union, the Army's commanding officer, General Winfield Scott, called Lee to Washington. There, Lincoln offered him command of Union forces for the upcoming Civil War. In subsequent days at home across the Potomac River at Arlington, Lee wrestled with his decision. He was against secession, and he had left directions in his will to free all the slaves he and his wife had inherited from her father. Having graduated with highest honors from West Point, he had served his country with honor during the Mexican War and in the peace that followed. But when Virginia left the Union, Lee determined not to draw his sword against his native state. He graciously declined Lincoln's offer.

Lee volunteered to serve in the Virginia militia, and soon, Confederate president Jefferson Davis made Lee his military aide. When the commander of the Confederate army defending Richmond was wounded in June 1862, Lee was given command, renaming his troops "the Army of Northern Virginia." Few people anticipated that this quiet, reserved man would become one of the greatest warriors in the history of the world. In fact, Union general McClelland, whose forces were only a few miles away, believed that Lee would prove too timid to lead an army in the field. In the next three years, however, Lee won battle after battle through daring marches and audacious strategies, even though his army was continually outmanned, outgunned, underfed, and poorly clothed.

Lee's impact on his men wasn't limited to respect for his military prowess. A deeply spiritual man, Lee was also revered for his walk with God. In fact, a spiritual awakening that swept not only the Army of Northern Virginia, but the entire South during the winter of '63–64 can be traced to the influence of two Christian warriors. Lee was one of them. (Stonewall Jackson was the other.)

Attrition severely depleted the Southern army, and by April 1865, military brilliance couldn't overcome the lack of men, powder, and food. After a final, valiant attempt to break away from Union forces, Lee surrendered to General Grant at Appomattox Court House and went home to his invalid wife, Mary.

In the days after the surrender at Appomattox, soldiers came by to see their beloved leader.

[One day a] tall ex-soldier in dusty, homespun attire came in and said, "General, I followed you for four years and done the best I knowed how. Me and my wife live on a little farm away up on Blue Ridge Mountains. If you will come up thar we will take care of you the best we know how as long as we live." Lee took both of the man's hands in his own. Tears ran down his cheeks. He thanked the man and offered him a suit someone had given him.[1]

Soon after that, an insurance company offered Lee a salary of $50,000 a year for the use of his name. Because he wasn't familiar with the business, Lee declined.

"But, General," the businessman explained, "you will not be expected to do any work. What we wish is the use of your name."

Lee replied indignantly, "Don't you think that if my name is worth $50,000 a year, I ought to be very careful about taking care of it?"

Instead, he accepted the offer to become president of bankrupt Washington College for a salary of $1,500 a year because he wanted to help young men, many of whom had been in his army only months before. Having served

> *"Don't you think that if my name is worth $50,000 a year, I ought to be very careful about taking care of it?"*

as adjutant at West Point years prior to the Civil War, he knew what a good education could mean to these young men, especially as the South tried to rebuild.

As president, Lee brought an innovative concept to Washington College: elective courses. And because of his creativity, not to mention his reputation, his students' respect for him bordered on idol worship.

From time to time, a student who was failing to live up to Lee's expectations would receive a summons to the president's office. There, Lee would gently but firmly remind the lad (usually one who was too young to have served in Lee's army) of the benefits of an education, and then ask for a commitment to improvement. These little talks rarely failed to inspire the student to recovery. Why? Because Lee's own integrity and experience lent *credence* to every word he said. In other words, he had *earned* the right to be heard. And people listened because he was credible.

If we want people to listen—and to be inspired—then we, too, must earn the right to be heard. Like General Lee, we must be *credible*.

CREDIBILITY: THE QUALITY OR POWER OF INSPIRING BELIEF

(Merriam-Webster's Collegiate Dictionary, 11th ed.)

Ingredients

As seen in the life of Robert E. Lee, credibility is a blend of several important ingredients that convincingly communicate, "I've been there. I know what I'm talking about, and I know what you're going through. When I offer to help, you can trust me." Let's look at the components that allow you to speak with authority.

Intellectual credibility —

In today's society, we are often impressed by a person's résumé and the degrees listed there. At the same time, though, we instinctively realize that one's intellect goes far beyond a list of letters after his or her name. Some of the greatest leaders, such as Abraham Lincoln, were self-taught. They had nimble, open, inquisitive minds, and they earned the right to be heard because of their wealth of *experience.* But whether their knowledge comes from the classroom or the "school of hard knocks," we respect people who know what they're talking about —especially if they don't try to impress us. People like this possess *intellectual credibility.* They aren't threatened by others' questions, so they answer them with honesty. If they don't know the answer, they admit it and do whatever it takes to find it.

Moral credibility —

Too often in our culture, we tolerate destructive behavior in ourselves and are entertained by the sins of others. In this environment, a truly moral person stands out tall and strong. She rejects deceit and corruption. She treasures honesty and decency. She is a person of *moral credibility.*

Morally credible people don't flaunt their purity and delight in condemning those who fail. They instead befriend the fallen, just as Christ did. Jesus was a true "friend of sinners" (see Matthew 11:19

and Luke 7:34). Even those whose morals were rocky knew that He loved and accepted them. And His gracious, unpretentious love, coupled with his uncompromised morals, made him eternally credible. As such, He inspired and changed many lives — including mine.

Relational credibility —

Most of the time, we know who is trustworthy and who should be tested again before we trust them. Those we choose to trust fully are typically those individuals who possess *relational credibility,* that is, repute they've earned based on their relationships with us. Relational credibility doesn't produce blind loyalty; rather, it is grown out of a person's reputation for telling the truth and doing so in a way that is most helpful to the hearer. People who demonstrate relational credibility never use people; on the contrary, they have our best interests at heart, and we know it.

When I think of people who exude relational credibility, my friend Victor Oliver is top on my list. Victor is an executive at a major publishing company, and for the last five years, I've spent time with him in business meetings, at coffee shops, on the golf course, and in every other conceivable situation. I've watched him relate to corporate executives, and I've seen him interact with punk rock–loving, Gothic baristas. In every encounter, Victor gives each individual undistracted attention. His demeanor, eye contact, and words communicate, "You are important to me." People sense it, and they instantly trust him. I've seen tears well up in people's eyes simply because Victor communicated grace to them. Perhaps he's the only one who has demonstrated that he truly cares, and they soak it up, suddenly unafraid to show their emotions. Why? Because in every relationship, be it close or casual, it is clear that he is *genuine.* Above all things, Victor is a man of truth. In fact, he has said some hard things to me that I wouldn't have accepted from anyone else. And I listened.

Truth and grace: these are the mark of Victor Oliver — and of *anyone* with relational credibility.

Emotional credibility –

We earn respect when we are honest with ourselves about the full range of our emotions and appropriately communicate them to others. Many people are afraid of losing control of their explosive feelings, so they keep the lid on tight, increasing the pressure and producing an even bigger explosion later. On the other hand, some people express more emotions than others care to know about! They wear their feelings on their sleeves – and on our sleeves too. But those who are balanced, suitably sharing and controlling their emotions, earn *emotional credibility*. We trust them because they are on an even keel. We're not fearful of sudden, unpredictable outbursts or random displays of emotion. Emotionally credible people are even-tempered, but they're also honest about their anger, hurts, doubts, fears, and dreams – and they inspire us to be honest about ours.

> *We earn respect when we are honest with ourselves about the full range of our emotions and appropriately communicate them to others.*

Experiential credibility –

The Confederate president trusted Lee as a soldier because Lee had experience commanding troops both in combat and in peacetime. Washington College trusted him to be president of their little school because as adjutant of West Point, he had earned a sterling reputation as a leader. But when Lee was offered an exorbitant salary in a field in which he had no experience, he turned it down. He was a model of *experiential credibility*. We trust credentials to a certain degree, but even more, we trust experience. The recommendation of a friend who tells us, "This attorney did a great job for me," will go a lot farther than any curriculum vitae. People lose damage their experiential credibility when they pretend to have knowledge that they don't really have. Lee wouldn't do it. You shouldn't either.

These traits form a matrix of credibility, but none of us gets a 10 out of 10 in all categories. King David was an incredible military commander with astute political instincts, but his moral failures crippled his reign. Robert E. Lee has been idolized for generations, yet he was too dominating in the lives of his daughters, who never married.

Even so, both men successfully inspired those around them. You can do the same, and you don't have to be perfect to do so. You just have to be, as best you can, a person others can *believe* in. You'll make mistakes, and in some areas your credibility may be tarnished. But if others see you, by and large, as a person of *integrity*, then the good in you will serve as inspiration to those who need your example.

ERODING CREDIBILITY

To review, any leader, whether of a corporation or a house full of teenagers, earns the right to speak by being trustworthy in the areas we just examined:

- When people trust our intellect, they'll be inspired to listen when we make personal or professional recommendations. (Intellectual Credibility)
- When they trust our morals, they know that our motives are pure. We're not "out to get them"; instead, we've got their best interests at heart. (Moral Credibility)
- When they're confident in their relationship with us, they're unafraid to step out and take progressive actions. (Relational Credibility)
- If we have demonstrated emotional stability, they won't constantly be in second-guess mode: *What if I make a mistake? Will she blow her top? Will I get fired? Will he pick someone else?* (Emotional Credibility) That's hardly a recipe for inspiration. And finally . . .
- When we can point to hard-won experience, those we lead are confident that we know what we're talking about. To follow our lead, then, is natural, not contrived. (Experiential Credibility)

In essence, then, our credibility serves as a catalyst to inspire others to take action — by choice.

Unfortunately, many leaders just can't be trusted. And even if they start out well, they end up being like the boss I mentioned earlier. She led me to believe I was on an executive trajectory; but instead, she just wanted a chauffeur. Or, remember Will's boss, the one who got his jollies at the expense of his "underlings"? Any honor that he bestowed was given superficially, because *he* was the star. As leaders continue to exhibit behaviors such as these, their credibility gradually (or rapidly) erodes. Employees no longer trust them, and the whole atmosphere is drained of inspiration. With their own trust shattered and their people's inspiration derailed, leaders are left with only one option: trying to control their staff. In businesses, the currency of control consists of salaries, bonuses, promotions, titles, awards, mention in company newsletters, opportunities to make presentations at corporate events, desirable accounts, corner offices, and similar perks. All of these things can be used by credible, competent managers to affirm employees for a job well done, but in the hands of leaders who lack credibility, they are tools to control people's behavior for selfish purposes. The difference is in the motive, and shrewd employees can detect the difference.

A few years ago, I served as a consultant for a large ad agency in the Midwest. The CEO was a very bright guy who had tremendous business savvy, but rumors leaked out about his handling of company finances. Like many CEOs, he used promotions and bonuses to reward his favorite VPs, but the problem was that the bonuses didn't seem to have any correlation with performance. That raised suspicion, especially among the VPs who received less than they felt they deserved. As always, unmet expectations soon led to resentment. Not long after that, the company experienced financial difficulties, but another rumor leaked out: Though no bonuses would be paid to any of the employees, both the CEO and the CFO received hefty checks. Suspicion and resentment then escalated to deep distrust and outright rebellion. The company continued to experience problems, and they had to be downsized. Several of the VPs who felt their unscrupulous CEO had cheated them out of their rightful bonuses took this opportunity to resign and start new companies. Some of these companies became chief competitors and almost drove the original company out of business. In this case, a leader's selfishness and financial mismanagement created such bad blood that it severely crippled the company. To this day, the company has never recovered.

THE COST OF A CREDIBILITY DEFICIT

The lack of credibility costs corporate America in many different ways, from the impact of elevated staff stress levels to increased costs of doing business due to new federal regulations to prevent mismanagement. After the Enron debacle, Congress passed the Sarbanes-Oxley Act of 2002 to clamp down on corporate fraud. If you think that didn't cost corporate America, consider this: According to Stephen M. R. Covey in *The Speed of Trust,* "the cost of implementing one section alone [of Sarbanes-Oxley] [was] $35 billion, exceeding the original SEC estimate by 28 times."[2] These costs, of course, will be passed along to consumers — and all because of the lack of corporate credibility.

What about the costs on the home front? When parents lose credibility *at home,* what can they expect? Going back to *Merriam-Webster's* definition of credibility, once parents squander their "power of inspiring belief," they begin to lose power of *every* kind. What do I mean?

Parents are wasting their breath when they tell their children not to smoke even as they themselves light up. If they wanted to inspire their teens to be nonsmokers, they just failed. Similarly, when mom and dad barely make it home from the bar, yet they tell their own son not to drink, oh, they inspire him all right — to rebel. And parents who want to motivate their children to be honest will never succeed when they themselves play loose with the facts. In all three cases, not only has the power to inspire belief been lost, but the power to persuade *in general* has been compromised. Parents, at every point that our kids see a disconnect between our words and our actions, our credibility gap widens. The price? We lose their respect. We risk disobedience and even open rebellion. And their confidence in our word may never be restored. Where once we could *inspire*, we now have to *compel*. It's a high price to pay for not being credible.

If, on the other hand, our children observe that we "walk the talk," that is, our words and our actions are consistent, we build credibility, and we inspire our children. Dad, your son will say, "I want to be *just like him*." Mom, your daughter will begin to mimic every good quality she sees in you. Why? Because your children have rung up your words on the counter of their experience and accepted them as *credible*. They will not hesitate to follow your example. And speaking of example . . .

YOUR EXAMPLE MEANS EVERYTHING

A few months ago, I was meeting in Nashville with Dan Cathy, the son of Truett Cathy, founder of Chick-fil-A. Dan is now the president and CEO of the very successful company, and it's not hard to see why.

The day we met, Dan did something most CEOs would never do. As our party began getting into a van to go to a meeting, we discovered that there wasn't quite enough room for everybody. Instantly, Dan jumped out, saying only, "Take my seat," to the person standing outside. Dan then walked to the back of the van and got in with the luggage. He didn't make a big deal of it. There was no image he was trying to project or protect. Dan was just being himself. He lives to serve others, and this was simply one moment among many of selfless service in a lifestyle of caring for others. Do people around him notice? You bet. Are they affected? Profoundly. Leaders should never expect people to do anything they aren't willing to do. Dan doesn't. He is more than willing to do anything that he asks his employees to do—and they know it. I wonder how many people will be inspired to imitate his actions in the years to come . . .

CREDIBILITY: A SUMMARY

Trust is a precious but fragile commodity. Where it grows in relationships, people experience the wonderful blend of contentment and zeal, but where it is eroded, stress levels rise and suspicions rule, both at the office and at home. We simply can't inspire people who don't trust us. We may be able to control them, but we can't truly inspire them.

> *We simply can't inspire people who don't trust us. We may be able to control them, but we can't truly inspire them.*

We can never demand that people trust us. We earn the right to be believed, one moment at a time — at home, at the coffee shop, on the warehouse floor, in the boardroom . . . or in a van, on the way to a meeting. All day, every day, we have countless opportunities to either build or erode our credibility with the people around us.

Which choice will you make?

THINK ABOUT IT . . .

1. Who are some people (write in code here) that at first you thought were trustworthy, but you found out later were not? How did you feel around each of these persons before the revelation? after it?

2. Give yourself a score of 0 (abysmal) to 10 (you are the model) in these areas of credibility:
   — Intellectual:

   — Moral:

   — Relational:

   — Emotional:

   — Experiential:

   Which one is a strength? Which one needs some improvement? What will you do about it?

GOING DEEPER

For this exercise, you'll need several pieces of paper, or if you use a journal to record your thoughts, you can write in it. Don't rush through this. Take your time to identify significant moments in relationships and consider the impact of those moments on your life.

1. Write your own "trust history" and identify the patterns in your life of blind trust, distrust, and perceptive trust.

    — Who were the trustworthy people in your life?

    — How did they affect you?

    — How old were you when you were around them?

    — Who were the untrustworthy people in your life?

    — How did they affect you?

2. Who are the people in your life now who are generally trustworthy?
   — Describe these relationships.

   — How do they affect you?

3. Who are the people in your life now who are generally untrustworthy?
   — Describe these relationships.

   — How do they affect you?

4. What would your best friends say about your trustworthiness?

5. What would those who report to you say about your trustworthiness?

6. From this exercise, what conclusions do you draw about your own ability to trust perceptively and others' willingness to trust you?

7. To determine if and to what degree others perceive you as trustworthy and credible, use the 360 Profile from the previous chapter. In the analysis, don't rush to defend yourself. Accept compliments and correction with equal grace.

5 Inspire with Great Stories — Yours and Theirs

"You have to understand, my dears, that the shortest distance between truth and a human being is a story."
– *Anthony de Mello, from* One Minute Wisdom

"Story," wrote author and educator Tim Trelease, "is the vehicle we use to make sense of our lives in a world that often defies logic."

Ah, stories. We love them. Nothing can capture our hearts like a good story. It should come as no surprise, then, that the most inspiring people in history were those who told gripping stories. Two of my favorites are Mark Twain and Ronald Reagan. Whatever we may think of their personal lives or their politics, these men impacted millions . . . by telling *stories*.

Skillfully woven stories often become the fodder for blockbuster movies. And what makes them blockbusters instead of B movies is their ability to move us. Some of their storylines move us to anger; others to melancholy; and still others, to frivolity. Some of us are stirred by the courage of the men in *Black Hawk Down*; others of us are inspired by the love and loyalty of the sisters in *Sense and Sensibility*. But though we may differ from our spouses — and from each other — in the movies we each prefer, at the core, we *all* gravitate toward those with storylines that touch our hearts — and we remember them. We may forget our first-grade teacher's name, what we wore on our first date — even what we had for dinner last night—but we will never forget a meaningful story told well. In fact, when people have long forgotten *my* name, they'll remember the stories I told them. Why? Because there's power in story. If you are a great inspirer, you already know this.

THE POWER OF STORIES

Great leaders tell great stories. They understand that stories are among their greatest resources for inspiring those under them. Sometimes they craft and communicate their own tales. Other times, they draw on the experiences of others. But either way, a great leader telling a great story will touch hearts and change lives.

A meaningful story can make the difference between a boring meeting and one that the staff eagerly anticipates, between an ineffective teacher-student conference and a productive one, between a father-son talk that works and one that doesn't. Sadly, many people either don't understand the power of stories or don't expend the effort to craft them for the people they lead.

STORYTELLING WORKS

Stories can be effectively used in virtually every context, with or without props or visual aids. Further, you don't have to be a master communicator to tell effective stories. You simply have to tell stories that capture *your* interest and motivate *you*. If you're moved by it, then it's likely that you'll tell it in a way that moves others. It's that simple.

If you're moved by it, then it's likely that you'll tell it in a way that moves others.

People who inspire others tell stories to:

- teach life lessons,
- keep important traditions alive,
- say hard-to-hear things,
- share vision,
- rally a team together, and
- connect with the soul of another person or even the soul of an audience.

Some people, though, won't even try. They hide behind the excuse that they're not "gifted" speakers. But if you have a pulse, you can be an effective storyteller. It may be rough at first, but just as you refine any other ability, you can improve your storytelling skills. You know the cliché: Practice makes perfect. As you learn the craft, you'll find that particular types of stories fit your personality better than others and that you enjoy telling some more than others. Ultimately, you'll develop an entire repertoire of stories to tell at appropriate times to reinforce certain points, and you'll always be hunting for more stories that you can use to inspire people around you.

FINDING A STORY

I firmly believe that every person I meet has a great story to tell— in fact, most people have lots of them. I often go exploring. Once I know people in more than a superficial way, I ask them to tell me about themselves and the paths of their lives' journeys. I don't pry. I just ask a simple question or two, and in many cases, great stories tumble out. Some people have thought long and hard about the lessons they've learned from failures, rejection, illness, and other heartbreaking circumstances. They've already done the work of reflection, and the lessons they've discovered shape every aspect of their lives. They can now use this wisdom to inspire others.

But occasionally, right in the middle of telling me their stories, only then does it dawn on them what they were meant to learn from their experiences. In more than a few serendipitous instances, people's eyes have lit up as they suddenly drew the most important conclusions of their lives from the stories they *just told me*. And from that moment on, those conclusions would be sources of inspiration for all who knew them.

So, what's your story? And more important, how can you tell it so that it inspires another?

YOUR OWN STORY

The same things that make the storylines of major motion pictures work apply to our own stories as well. Like any edge-of-your-seat movie, our lives are in constant motion. They aren't static, unbroken lines of sameness. In our pasts, we have each encountered turning points, moments when we came face to face with difficult decisions, and the choices we made determined the course of our lives. Some of these were very natural stages experienced by all, such as college and career choices; geographical or professional moves; and births, marriages, and deaths. At other times, though, we faced unexpected (and unwanted) circumstances that tested our values and courage. These defining moments — ones that stopped us in our tracks and caused us to reevaluate our direction in life — filled our lives with irony. Perhaps we didn't make great decisions at the outset. We stumbled through doubts, depression, fatigue, and failure, but in the end, we found fresh springs of hope. From weakness sprang strength; from failure, success; from rejection, love; and from discouragement, the will to go on. Today these stories define us — and give us a wonderful platform for inspiring others. In fact, *all* difficult events in our lives, even those that didn't turn out well, can be powerfully inspiring if we can find a "moral" or two in them and convey those hard-won lessons through the power of story.

Here are some tips for fashioning stories that will inspire those around you.

CRAFTING GREAT STORIES

First, examine your own life.

Most of us think our lives are dull and boring, but they aren't. We just need a little effort to remember details and dig for lessons learned. Look through old annuals, scrapbooks, or photo albums. The images will jog your memory and remind you of events long forgotten, but rich with lessons you learned — or that you should have learned. Talk to those who were with you during those times to make sure you have your facts straight and to offer insights that you may have missed. Think about the happiest times in your life, but don't focus only on that which was good. Experiences both positive and negative are the stuff of life, and often, those experiences that were the very worst ultimately led to what was best for each of us. So also reflect on periods of hardship, sickness, and loss. Then, as you narrate, let your listeners feel your pain. Milk the moments when you had no idea what to do next, when all hope seemed lost, when there was seemingly no light at the end of the tunnel, when the situation was less-than-ideal. See, great stories aren't based on the superficial image of an ideal life — they depict our heroic choices to face reality and find hope instead of despair.

Look for great stories everywhere you go.

We develop habits to reinforce things we believe are important, and looking for inspiring stories can be like any other habit we cultivate. If you know you need a story to use with your team or family, you'll have your antennae up. When you read the newspaper, you'll notice stories of courage, creativity, endurance, or stupidity. You'll listen to Paul Harvey or read books that have gripping narratives. You'll ask people questions about the funniest points in their lives or their pivotal moments. You'll write down important stories, you'll clip them out of the newspaper, and you'll copy them from the Internet. (You can find many riveting stories to inspire you, your staff, and your family, at inspirationblvd.com. Look under "Defining Moments.")

Make sure your story has a point.

A truly inspirational story communicates a lesson that inspires or warns. Sometimes the lesson is intuitively obvious, but in a few cases, we have to dig a little deeper to find a richer vein of meaning.

Here's a story to inspire you. Read it and see if you can find the lesson.

If anyone ever had a reason to use her family background as an excuse for self-pity and passivity, Elizabeth did. She grew up in one of the most tumultuous, bitter families known to history. Her father, Henry VIII of England, had discarded each of his wives, one by one, when she failed to produce male heirs. His first wife, Catherine of Aragon, gave him only a daughter, Mary. Henry demanded a divorce. When the Catholic Church told him no, he chose an archbishop who would grant the divorce and then founded his own church, the Church of England—of which he conveniently declared himself to be the head.

After the divorce, the woman of his dreams, Anne Boleyn, became pregnant, and Henry was sure he finally had an heir. Anne, though, gave the disappointed king another girl—this time, Elizabeth. After her birth, Anne was unable to have another child, so Henry had her beheaded when Elizabeth was just three years old. She grew up without a mother. Worse, once her mother was dead, Henry declared her illegitimate.

Henry's pursuit of a son eventually led him to marry six wives, but none gave him the son he desperately wanted. After his death, a nephew, Edward VI, became king and immediately placed Elizabeth in confinement. But soon, that king died, and Elizabeth's half sister, Mary, took the throne.

Mary was a devout Catholic determined to return the "true faith," that of her discarded mother, back to England. She was so ruthless in her efforts that she earned the moniker "Bloody Mary," as her rule was marked by recriminations against anyone who failed to support her cause. Elizabeth herself was accused of supporting Protestants, and, again, she was imprisoned. It would have been a very good time for Elizabeth to give up.

But she didn't. During those years of imprisonment, Elizabeth studied and trained—hard—for the day that she herself might come to power.

Eventually, Mary became sick and died, and Elizabeth became Queen of England. What a blessing, right? Well . . . not exactly.

Elizabeth inherited a country that was on the brink of civil war, with fear and distrust creating an elaborate network of open and secret alliances. A once mighty nation had lost power and stature among the nations on the continent. Yet in a world of powerful men, this frail, delicate woman began one of the most remarkable reigns in history.

Elizabeth proved to be a shrewd judge of character and a visionary in world affairs. She supported the adventures of explorer Walter Raleigh and seafarer Francis Drake, who thrilled the nation by sailing around the world not long after Magellan's historic and tragic voyage. At home, she provided stability, and trade flourished. Full pockets enabled old animosities to subside. And the arts saw a renaissance such as England had never seen. The Elizabethan Age was the time of Shakespeare and the Globe Theater, and Sir Isaac Newton's discoveries and theories delighted the academies.

But trouble was brewing. Early in her reign, Elizabeth had turned down a marriage proposal from Phillip II of Spain. And years later, when she sent her closest friend, Robert Dudley, to lead an army to support the Dutch against Spain's domination, Dudley proved to be an incompetent military leader. The army returned home in shame.

Intent upon revenge — both military and romantic — Phillip sailed his fleet of incomparable ships, the Spanish Armada, into English waters in 1588. England knew they could only muster a few small boats against the mightiest fleet ever known, but they sailed out to face them anyway — with an ingenious plan: they would set some of their own ships on fire, then let the wind carry them right into the far bigger Spanish ships.

And that's exactly what they did. Though the Spaniards' ships were equipped with row after row of cannon, their size prevented quick maneuvering as they burned uncontrollably. Among the blazing monstrosities, the small and nimble English warships darted in and out with ease, firing their cannon again and again at the unsuspecting and bewildered Spaniards. To the utter astonishment of all of Europe, the English won the day!

But on the mainland the Queen didn't comprehend the enormity of her fleet's victory. So, expecting an invasion by Spain, she herself led her little army to the plains of southeast England to await the Spanish soldiers. Once at Essex, Elizabeth stepped up to address her troops and lead them in battle. Wearing a silver breastplate over a white velvet dress, Elizabeth quieted the men and then said, "My loving people, we have been persuaded by some that are careful of our safety, to take heed how we commit ourself to armed multitudes for fear of treachery; but I assure you, I do not desire to live to distrust my faithful and loving people . . . I know I have the body but of a weak and feeble woman, but I have the heart and stomach of a king, and of a King of England too, and think foul scorn that Parma or Spain, or any Prince of Europe should dare to invade the borders of my realm."

The invasion never came, and the Queen and her people soon realized they had won one of the most dramatic military victories in history. The celebration at St. Paul's in London rivaled her coronation in the effusion of joy and thanksgiving.

Elizabeth presided over perhaps the most prosperous years of England's storied history. She transformed a tattered nation into one that wielded power in every field of civilization: the arts, politics, trade, exploration, and military might. And though Elizabeth lived four centuries before women's lib, she exemplified leadership on the grandest scale.

What a story! Though Elizabeth could have languished in her cell, all hope lost, she chose to maintain a positive outlook, using her time of incarceration to build character and intelligence for a future she never stopped believing would come. When she emerged, she was ready to take on the world. In time, she became an example to everyone around her — to entire nations of people who have since praised and emulated her courage. Now, that's an inspiring tale!

Focus on the main points, and deliver the point with a punch.

We've all heard speakers ramble on as they told detail after detail of a story that seemed to go on for eternity. At first, we were interested, because all stories promise a meaningful ending, but after a while, boredom killed our hopes. In informal settings, stories don't need a lot of preparation, but if you are speaking to an audience or you plan to use a story multiple times, craft it carefully. Know in advance the first line you want to say. You may want to begin by asking a thought-provoking question. However you choose to begin, though, memorize and practice that opening line. It's hard to bring a story to a solid conclusion when you start out shaky.

After your strong start, keep your story flowing as you make your main points, adding colorful details to make the story come alive. Push your listeners' "hot buttons" as you narrate. Remember, you are endeavoring to inspire them. By now you should know some of their dreams and goals. How can your story speak to those aspirations? Look for ways to direct your story to their innermost yearnings.

And don't forget the element of surprise. Great stories inevitably contain one, something that brings us to the edge of our seats. Novelist Flannery O'Connor reflected, "From my own experience in trying to make stories 'work,' I have discovered that what is needed is an action that is totally unexpected, yet totally believable, and I have found that, for me, this is always an action which indicates that grace has been offered. And frequently it is an action in which the devil has been the unwilling instrument of grace. This is not a piece of knowledge that I consciously put into my stories;

When you tell a story, take advantage of the element of surprise, and use it to inspire your listeners

it is a discovery that I get out of them."[1] Sounds like life, like the many times people had a prearranged plan—and then it came to a grinding halt, and they were forced to make a pivotal decision. No one has to consciously place surprise in anyone's life. It is, as O'Connor put it, "a discovery." When you tell a story, take advantage of the element of surprise, and use it to inspire your listeners.

Finally, deliver the punch line boldly and clearly. Then *stop*. Don't explain the point ad infinitum (or ad nauseum!). State it once, state it clearly, and say it like you mean it. Then move on to the next thing on the agenda.

Be authentic in applying the lesson to your own life.

Obviously, if the story is about your experiences, it will be relatively easy to be genuine as you communicate the application. But always dig a little deeper to look for added meaning. Don't make something up just to sound profound, but ask the "why" questions and the "what next" questions. Talk about the story with your spouse or a good friend. He or she may recall that the experience has shaped your life more deeply or in a different way than you remembered.

If the story is told in third person, make sure to connect the dots for people who are listening. Relate the lesson to your own life by saying, "This is what this story says to me," or "Here's how I have applied [or will apply] the moral of this story." In any inspirational message, the "so what?" at the end is as essential as the details of the story. Don't rush past this crucial element! Take your time to craft your application statement so that the lights come on, heads nod, and people think, *I can do that, too! In fact, I've got to do that!*

When you communicate the lesson and your application of it to your life, you open your heart a bit for others to see. That makes you real and approachable, but there's a risk too. Some of us think,

Oh, no. I've opened up and told everyone about my embarrassing mistake. Now they know I'm not 'all that'! News flash: *They already knew it.* They just wanted to see if you would admit it.

If possible, use the story and the "so what?" application as a jumping-off point for discussion.

Your team, friends, or family will benefit from dialogue about the lesson of the story. In many cases, the story itself will bring up memories, desires, and goals — perhaps long buried but now resurrected. Ask open-ended questions that stimulate reflection and don't have simple answers, for instance, "Why do you think he did that?" or "How would you have responded in the same situation?" And when people answer, don't jump in to challenge or correct them. Allow them to have different perspectives and arrive at dissimilar conclusions. Sometimes, people offer opposing views to see if you can be trusted. Don't overreact, and don't be defensive. Stay calm and ask them to tell you more of their perceptions.

STORYTELLING IS FOR ALL OF US

Some of us are natural storytellers, and we have the innate ability to weave a tale that captivates people. Coaches and Innovators, for instance, are often quite at ease telling stories. Coaches enjoy talking about teams coming together to accomplish great things. Innovators might tell how someone faced a difficult problem and found a solution that changed thousands of lives. Commanders excel at telling stories about people who courageously faced seemingly insurmountable challenges and overcame incredible obstacles. Accountability Partners might explain how a single person's attention to detail made the difference between success and failure for a team or a company. But no matter what the leadership style, *all* of us can learn to tell stories that inspire people, and with a little practice using the tips I just offered, we can only get better with time.

I once coached a CEO of a large New York corporation in how to uncover and communicate inspiring stories. Though this gentleman was very bright, he lacked the confidence to make inspiring presentations. In our early conversations, I remember asking him a number of questions to find out what interested him. I soon learned that he is an avid pro football fan. He is especially enamored with legendary Cowboys coach Tom Landry. This CEO had studied Landry's life and was impressed with his skill in selecting, motivating, and coaching his players. When he told me stories of Landry's leadership, his eyes lit up and he became more animated than I had ever seen him. I recognized instantly his best source of inspiration.

Together, this CEO and I identified several noteworthy stories (like the tale of the famous "Ice Bowl" between Dallas and Green Bay) that he could use in his presentations to his top executives and stockholders. We discussed the lessons he learned from each story, and then crafted the wording so that he could speak eloquently about how those lessons shaped his own life. And it worked.

Now, all of that was already there, but this leader had just never put the pieces together before in a way that he could use to inspire others. Today, when he speaks at such events, his past dread is replaced by genuine excitement. He is confident that he will connect with his audience — and he does.

In Summary

Anytime you are in front of your team, stockholders, constituents, a class, your family, or anyone else you hope to inspire as you impart information, always — *always* — begin with a story. People remember the mental images generated by our stories far better than they do facts, figures, and charts. The greatest communicator of all time, Jesus of Nazareth, could have overwhelmed people with his vast, divine knowledge, but time after time, He told parables — *stories* — that captured people's hearts, communicated His message through narrative, and *inspired* them.

People remember the mental images generated by our stories far better than they do facts, figures, and charts.

Think for a moment about the amazing success of a little periodical known as *Guideposts*. This publication is a hit precisely because of the inspirational *stories* found on every page. And one of the publishing marvels of recent decades is the Chicken Soup series, which are — what? Collections of stories that make us laugh, cry, and sigh.

Even in the high-pressure world of big business, top consultants are helping corporate executives realize the power of stories. Quoting Harvard psychologist Howard Gardner, Tom Peters wrote in *Leading Minds*, "A key, perhaps the key, to leadership is . . . the effective communication of a story."[2] Peters then added, "Whether your gig involves primitive tribes or corporate tribes . . . is the (often unsung) Power of Storytelling. It was true in the bush. It's true in the boardroom. And it's true everywhere in between."[3]

Not long ago, I was working with a team, and one of their newest employees hesitated to make decisions and take action. Her supervisor had become very frustrated and gave her rules and deadlines to force her to take action, but nothing changed. I sat down with her, and I told her about an experience I had when I was learning to fly. I had flown several times with my instructor, and on this day before we left the hangar, he told me that he wanted me to take control of the plane from take off to landing. He assured me that he'd be sitting right next to me the whole time. We got in the single-engine plane and taxied out to the runway. I sat waiting for his instructions, but he just sat there looking straight ahead. We sat and sat. A couple of planes lined up behind us, but still, we just sat there. Finally, I turned to him to ask him what he wanted me to do, but before I could speak, he said, "Terry, you're the pilot. Fly the plane." I immediately pushed the throttle forward and we took off. As I told the story, I prepared to share the lesson with the hesitant employee, but before I could say another word, she looked at me and said, "Terry, I know. I've got to fly this plane myself." I only smiled and nodded. From that moment, she became an effective, assertive team member.

Let me close this chapter with an admonition: If you are inexperienced or unsure about your ability to tell inspiring stories, *develop* the skills you need to speak well. What do you hope to achieve in the lives of those who need inspiration? Put forth a little effort to find stories to that end, developing a deep reservoir of gripping narratives that you can craft for your team or family and make a difference in their lives. You *can* become a good storyteller. And if you are already a good one, you can become a *great* one.

Start today.

THINK ABOUT IT . . .

1. What are your favorite movies? What do you like about them?

2. Who are the two or three best storytellers you know? What is the impact of their ability to craft and communicate great stories on you and others?

3. What is one story from your own life that you enjoy telling? Why do you enjoy it?

4. Review the tips under "Crafting Great Stories." Which of these do you do well? Which do you need to improve?

5. What is one thing you can do today or tomorrow to become a better storyteller?

Going Deeper

Take some time to carefully consider these exercises. Don't rush though them. Think long and hard about each one. For the rest of your life, you'll use the stories you define and the lessons you identify to touch people's lives.

1. Identify the most difficult moments or periods of your life.

— Are these your "defining moments"? Why or why not?

—What happened?

—How did they affect you at the time?

—What lessons did you learn then, or what lessons do you see now that you look back at those events?

2. Are there particular categories of events (such as sports, music, business, entertainment, or politics) that interest you? (If a story energizes you, you'll deliver it with enthusiasm and clarity. What do you read in your spare time? What part of the newspaper is most interesting to you? What do you talk about with your friends?) What are some stories in that category that you enjoy hearing and telling?

3. Select three stories from the first two exercises, either from your own life or from outside sources. Identify the specific lesson you draw from each one. In some cases, the lessons will be obvious, but in others, you'll want to dig a little to find the gold.

4. For each of the three stories and lessons, identify your personal application that makes it meaningful to you. This is the point at which the stories and the lessons become authentic in your experience and in your communication. Craft the "so what?" applications very carefully so you can state them clearly.

5. Create a readily accessible file for stories you tear out of the newspaper, copy from online sources, or jot down on napkins. As you become more sophisticated in your research, you can create separate files for different categories.

6. Take some time to finalize one story and present it to your team, staff, or family this week. In your preparation:

   —Select a story that energizes you.
   —Identify the main points in the story and enough details to make it interesting.
   —Underline or memorize your first line.
   —Identify the lesson or "moral" you want to communicate from the story.
   —Craft an authentic "so what?" application of the lesson to your own life.

   After you tell the story, its lesson, and your own application, ask your listeners an open-ended question about how they would have responded in the same situation or a similar question that elicits feedback.

7. On your weekly to-do sheet, add a regular item: Craft a story for the next meeting.

6 HELP PEOPLE LIVE ON PURPOSE

*"What man actually needs is not a tensionless state but rather
the striving and struggling for some goal worthy of him.
What he needs is not the discharge of tension at any cost,
but the call of a potential meaning waiting to be fulfilled by
him." – Victor Frankl, psychiatrist and survivor of a Nazi
concentration camp*

On July 20, 1985, Mel Fisher stood on the deck of his salvage boat,
off the Florida Keys. He and his crew were going through the same
routine they'd done a thousand times before. For seventeen years,
Fisher had been looking for a ship, the *Señora Nuestra de Atocha*, a
Spanish galleon that sank in a hurricane in 1622. The ship's manifest in Madrid described an almost unimaginable treasure—gold,
silver, and emeralds—so valuable that the Spanish empire went
into an economic depression when the news of the *Atocha's* sinking
was announced in court.

During those long years of looking for the ship, fate had not
been kind to Fisher. Ten years before, a diving accident claimed the
lives of his son and daughter-in-law. Money to fund the salvage operation ran out numerous times, and Fisher had to find additional
investors to bankroll the venture. Each time, another piece of the
pie left his grasp. Still, nothing could stop him from looking; he was
a man on a mission. And he knew it was there—somewhere—because he had been tantalizingly close on several occasions, finding
a gold necklace, a silver platter, and a cannon that was unmistakably from the ship.

On a hot July day, with years of failure behind them, the divers again rigged up a tube to the salvage boat's engines to blow sand off the bottom. But this time, when the sand cleared, the sight was what they had longed to find. One of the divers sprinted to the surface, ripped off his mask, and shouted, "It's here! We've found the main pile!"

The "main pile" was a stack of gold and silver bars six feet high, eight feet wide, and forty feet long. Scattered next to the stack were exquisitely crafted gold platters, candelabra, chains, and handfuls of the finest emeralds the New World had ever produced. That day, the men brought up so much treasure that the salvage boat threatened to sink. In the weeks that followed, they systematically cataloged every piece, from the smallest gold doubloon to the last gold bar. The value was estimated at $400 million.

On July 19, people in Key West had said Mel Fisher was a fool for pursuing his dream. On July 20, they hailed him as a genius.

BIGGER THAN OURSELVES

A sense of purpose gives meaning to our lives. It directs our choices, shapes our destiny, and gives us tenacity to keep going when others might quit. William James observed, "The greatest use of a life is to spend it for something that outlasts it." I couldn't agree more. For one's life to be truly significant, a person has to find something bigger than himself, a cause that he's convinced will make a difference in the world.

But in our society, people value externals, and the more the better. Worse, we live in an entitlement culture in which people not only take advantage of government welfare programs, but are convinced that they *deserve* those things that guarantee a fun, exciting, and easy life. And for most, the "good life" isn't a pursuit; it's a demand. When we don't get what we want, we whine, pout, and sue people's pants off. But the deceptive message that we are entitled to ever-increasing amounts of possessions and pleasure devastates our values and thwarts worthy purposes.

And yet, we amass. More, more, and evermore, we work hard to pursue not just assets, but success, promotions, money, sex, and power too. These things, we've been told, give us ultimate fulfillment. But it's a lie. When the circle of our lives is reduced to a dot, we realize (hopefully not too late) that there must be something more to life than wealth and amusement.

God has made each of us so that we can only be temporarily satisfied with self-absorption. Our golden "goods" may satisfy us for a while. But ultimately, the gold tarnishes and the glow of celebrity dims. If you don't believe it, listen to legendary automaker Lee Iacocca, who lamented, "Here I am in the twilight years of my life, still wondering what it's all about; I can tell you this: fame and fortune is for the birds," Or Walker Percy, the Southern "philosophical novelist," who said, "You can get all A's and still flunk life."

> *You can get all A's and still flunk life.*

Flunk life? How do you do that? By living without *purpose*.

In the last few years, a growing movement has been helping people find and pursue a compelling purpose. Rick Warren's *The Purpose Driven Life* has sold more than 20 million copies and has changed many lives. But we can't live on yesterday's insights and last year's meaning. We need to *keep* pursuing, *persist* in pushing, and *continue* clarifying the reason we get up each day—and then inspire others to do the same.

But how?

HAVE ONE, SHAPE ONE

A man who trains financial planners once told me that one of the biggest problems in his industry is financial planners who don't have their *own* plan. Such planners fail because their advice to their clients rings hollow. Their own lack of purpose has given them no personal experience they can use to convince *others* to pursue a purpose. The moral of this story is that we can't take someone to a place we've never been, and we can't help someone down a road we've never traveled. The first priority, then, for those of us who want to impart a compelling purpose is to have one for ourselves. A leader without a personal sense of purpose is a ship without a rudder. It drifts with the currents, no matter how hard the engine is running.

So, what's your purpose? That's a meaningless question unless you know what is important to you. To define the scope of your purpose, first look in the bed next to you, and in the room down the hall. What's there? Family.

Our families are treasures, worth every ounce of tenacity and energy their well-being requires. Living for their good is a no-brainer. We want them to be happy and fulfilled in life. Whatever their dreams, we want to inspire them and help them reach those dreams, because they are our flesh and blood.

Beyond family, many of us have also found (or are finding) a *cause* in which we invest a portion of our time, energy, and finances to make a difference in people's lives. A need touches our hearts, and we gladly devote ourselves to meeting it. Opportunities for such charitable undertakings are endless: AIDS relief in Africa, feeding hungry children through World Vision, building homes in our communities through Habitat for Humanity, women's shelters in every city, crisis pregnancy centers, caring for the elderly through Meals on Wheels, and countless other agencies meeting every kind of need in our neighborhoods, our nation, and around the planet. Some people choose to get involved in environmental concerns, politics, or youth character-building organizations, such as Boy Scouts and Girl Scouts. Even corporations are getting on the bandwagon. For example, Wal-Mart is organizing its employees' efforts to build houses and help in many other ways in their own communities. For many people, it's not enough to write a check. They want to invest some sweat too. It gives their lives *meaning*.

And then there is religion. We are spiritual creatures, and ultimately, we find our highest and most compelling meaning in a relationship with God. Whether we are Christians, Hindus, Muslims, or some other faith, most of us believe that Someone has a unique claim on our lives and calls us to the purpose of living according to our faith. In fact, wrote Os Guinness, "God calls us to himself so decisively that everything we are, everything we do, and everything we have is invested with a special devotion and dynamism lived out as a response to his summons and service."[1] That's purpose.

But even though our sense of purpose is God-given, the purpose itself — not to mention its realization — seldom comes to us on a silver platter. Finding our transcendent purpose involves rigorous pursuit, a few dead ends along the way,

> *But even though our sense of purpose is God-given, the purpose itself — not to mention its realization — seldom comes to us on a silver platter.*

and a growing sense that Someone else's valuation of our lives is far more important than all the pleasure and approval our culture promises. The path God chooses for us often twists and turns along the way, and ironically, the struggles of our early years can teach us life's most valuable lessons — and become the platform for our greatest impact in *others'* lives.

Václav Havel found his purpose in the crucible of suffering. A playwright and dissident in Communist Czechoslovakia, Havel was arrested and thrown into prison a total of four times, where he served years of hard labor for his "crimes" (speaking out for human rights). While imprisoned, he wrote a series of letters to his wife, later published as *Letters to Olga,* which delved into the daunting questions that haunted him: What is life about? What gives it meaning? And there, in the dehumanizing penal environment, Havel uncovered what was, for him, a signal insight: Responsibility is the key to our humanity. He wrote, "I would say that responsibility is a knife we use to carve our own inimitable features in the panorama of Being . . . Responsibility does establish identity, but we are not responsible because of our identity; instead, we have an identity because we are responsible . . . Human responsibility, as the word itself suggests, is responsibility to something."

Hmm . . . sounds like he's talking about purpose. Each of us, he's saying, is *responsible* to fulfill a purpose, to "carve out" our own features in the world and people around us through our individual missions in life. Havel certainly did. After his release from that prison cell, he became one of the most effective leaders in the last several decades. He led the Czech Republic out of the dark night of Communism and into the light of freedom and democracy. Needless to say, Havel inspired millions.

> *And that's exactly what we, as leaders, want to do: inspire those around us by finding our purpose — then helping them find and fulfill theirs as well.*

And that's exactly what we, as leaders, want to do: inspire those around us by finding our purpose — then helping them find and fulfill theirs as well.

COACHING PURPOSE

I've heard well-meaning speakers tell people that they should be able to write their purpose statement on the back of a business card. Well, *some* folks might be able to do that, but most can't, and the vast majority of us need time to grapple with the messy process of discovering what really makes us tick. Writing a purpose statement isn't something we can do in ten minutes after a talk. We might take a single step during that brief moment, but we demean the importance of the project if we see it as something to check off our to-do lists — or worse, something a speaker can check off his to-do list. Anytime someone offers a template that is essentially "one size fits all," then it probably inspires nobody.

People need to know that it's okay for them to be works in progress, without the pressure to come up with "the answer" for their futures in a rigid time frame. Of course, some use this freedom to procrastinate and put off meaningful decisions (if you notice this paralysis, address it boldly but lovingly), but most people genuinely want their lives to count. And you can help them.

The thing is, you can't *give* folks their purpose. For a mission to grip their hearts, they themselves have to work for it, struggle with it, and chisel it from the formless rock of their own lives. Shortcuts inevitably lead to shallow convictions and later, to disappointment. Identifying one's purpose can be very *hard* work, and it is up to the individual to do it.

But your role is crucial. You and I have the unmitigated privilege of walking beside others, pointing out their strengths, affirming their abilities, dreaming of possibilities with them, and helping them flesh out their purpose. You can, in fact, be instrumental in inspiring them to make their dreams, reality. But how do we even begin?

Paint a Picture

I like to use word pictures to communicate powerful messages of hope. For example, when I'm talking to an obvious Commander, I may say, "You're like a Special Forces captain who leads his men in the most difficult battlefield missions." He may not have realized what a strong leader he was. But remember, we inspire others when we recognize abilities in them that they don't see. You have just lit a fire for this Commander and perhaps helped him discover his purpose. To a pair of Innovators, I might say, "You two are just like Watson and Crick, the men who cracked the genetic code and unlocked all kinds of medical breakthroughs to help millions of people." Again, maybe these Innovators didn't know their ideas were so valuable. Might you have just inspired them to come up with more brilliant innovations? Could that be their *purpose?* Perhaps, and if so, they found it because of a picture *you* painted — with words.

We can use word pictures to connect with any audience. Martin Luther King Jr., were he alive today, could certainly attest to that. One of the most powerful and dramatic public messages in American history was his own "I have a dream" speech, delivered to more than two hundred thousand people from the steps of the Lincoln Memorial on August 28, 1963, at the height of the struggle for civil rights. Though King's talk lasted only seventeen minutes, the metaphors of freedom and hope inspired the nation — and they continue to inspire us today. Congressman John Lewis, who also spoke that day as one of the leaders of the civil rights movement, reflected on that day many years later: "Dr. King had the power, the ability and the capacity to transform those steps on the Lincoln Memorial into a modern day pulpit. By speaking the way he did, he educated, he inspired . . . not just the people there, but people throughout America and unborn generations."[2] And it's true. Though his own life was cut short, others whom Dr. King inspired found their purpose in carrying on the work that he had begun. You could, in fact, say he helped them *live on purpose*.

Tell on Yourself

I respect people whose lives are on a clear path to accomplishing something noble—but I *treasure* those who are willing to share with me how they arrived on that path. To inspire those around you to find and fulfill the purpose for their lives, share the story of the process you've gone through to clarify your own purpose. When I talk to people about their purpose, I share my journey with them as an example—certainly not a perfect one, but a genuine one. I tell them about my early attempts and how some of them worked out well. But I also explain that I've had enough dead ends to remind me that a compelling purpose in life is a gift to be cherished, never to be taken for granted.

> *I respect people whose lives are on a clear path to accomplishing something noble—but I treasure those who are willing to share with me how they arrived on that path.*

Like most people, I've made adjustments and clarified my purpose several times in my adult life. In fact, this book is a product of a reevaluation of my purpose. Though I've enjoyed what I've done in my life, over the last few years I've had a nagging feeling that I'm not in the center of the target. Over several months, I thought, prayed, talked to Debbi and a few close friends, and made some necessary midcourse corrections. Why? Because I want to have more impact on people. I want to equip leaders to be more effective — by inspiring those who look to them for leadership. And that's what this book is about. I'm telling on myself. And I'm pretty darned excited about it too!

Find Where the Roads Cross

As I meet with people and try to help them find their purpose, I look for the intersection of key elements: strengths, desires, dreams, and the company or organization's goals and available positions. If you are going to inspire anyone, particularly to live on purpose, you must connect with her dreams. We talked about this, in part, in principle #2. What does she want out of life? What are her goals for the immediate and distant future? The closer her personal objectives are aligned with the company's objectives and available opportunities, the more enthusiastic, effective, and fulfilled she will be, and the easier it will be to discover her own unique purpose.

Talk to each member of your team (and family) about how he or she can make a difference in others' lives in the next five years, ten years, and for a lifetime — a purpose. Then look at the dreams and aspirations each person cherishes. By now, you should know them, if you have practiced principle #2. See if these dreams can be tied in any way to the worthy purpose that each individual has unearthed. Then ask yourself, does this person have what it takes to fulfill this purpose, and most important, is she in the *right place* to pursue it? All of these elements are crucial, because once she reaches the place where she's living life on purpose, she is sailing the seas of inspiration.

Use Every Tool Available

The marketplace contains all kinds of resources that you can use to help people discover their purpose and to tailor their careers to fit their passions. Personality profiles, books, seminars, and articles are readily available, but your involvement is perhaps the most significant tool in the toolbox. Think about the resources that have helped you, and let those be the foundation for helping others. (To review several valuable resources to help people find their best fit, visit www.inspirationblvd.com.)

For me, Steven Covey's *The 7 Habits of Highly Effective People* was instrumental in my earliest attempts to clarify my purpose. One of the exercises he recommends has been copied by scores of consultants and presenters, because it is so effective. It sure worked for me. In the exercise, I imagined my own funeral, attended by my family, friends, and business associates. As I thought about what each one of them would say about me, the impact of my life at that moment became crystal clear—encouraging in some ways, but disheartening in others. I realized that I didn't have the kind of influence on some of my loved ones that I wanted to. I then imagined them saying the kinds of things I longed to hear about me. For example, I wanted my daughters to say, "My dad believed in me, and he helped me make my dreams come true." I wanted my mother and father to say, "We're so proud of Terry, because he truly loved us, and he devoted his life to something much bigger than himself." I wanted my employer to say, "I've never had anyone as dedicated, creative, and effective as Terry." The image of that scene next to my grave wasn't a dry academic exercise. It was a turning point. It captured my desires about the impact of my life, and I was more motivated and directed than ever to make necessary changes. And if this exercise inspired me, perhaps it will inspire you too—and all whom you hope to inspire.

Use the Best Tool of All

There are a lot of tools out there, some expensive, some not so pricey. But the best tool of the inspiration "trade" is *you*. Going back to principle #3, your finely tuned ability to see in others what they can't see for themselves is invaluable in helping them "find themselves" and then begin to live on *purpose,* using the best of what God gave them, to the best of their ability, to do the best that they can in life.

When I was an awkward kid, Larry Bone, whom I mentioned before, did exactly that. He saw something of value in me, and then, over many conversations, took the time to affirm my abilities — ones I didn't even realize I had! Not only that, but once Larry empowered me with a vision of my gifting, he encouraged me to live on purpose, using what he recognized in me to make a difference. My life has never been the same. Today, I want to "share the wealth." Just as Larry opened my eyes and gave me a sense of direction and purpose, I want to be the tool God uses to help others clarify their purpose for being and inspire them to live *intentionally*.

Don't you?

THINK ABOUT IT . . .

1. On a scale of 0 (not in the least) to 10 (crystal clear), how clearly defined and compelling is your sense of purpose? Explain your answer.

2. How can a person "get all A's and still flunk life"?

3. If your life stopped today, how would the world be different because you were alive?

4. What are some tools you've used to identify your purpose and live in the wheelhouse of effectiveness? What is the role of stories to inspire people to clarify their sense of purpose? What are some stories you can use?

5. What are some resources you can use to help others uncover and live by their sense of purpose?

6. What difference do you think it will make in the lives of the people you help to clarify their purpose in life? What difference will it make to you?

GOING DEEPER

Consider using these tools and exercises with the people who report to you.

1. Current impact—Imagine being an onlooker at your own funeral. Look for each family member, your best friends, and your business associates. List those people here, and write a summary of what you honestly believe they would say about you if they stood at your grave today (and took Sodium Pentothal to be sure they told the truth).

2. Strengths—What are some tools, such as personality inventories and ability assessments, that you can use to help people around you discover their reason-for-being and subsequently live on purpose? (See Principle #3 for one good idea.)

3. Desires — What are tools and exercises you can use to uncover and affirm people's passions? (See Principle #2 for suggestions.)

4. Opportunities — For each person, consider their abilities and desires, and then imagine what kind of impact this person can have in the next year, the next five years, and in his or her lifetime. With that in mind, discuss the possibilities that could help this take place. These possibilities become opportunities to consider. Bring in peers for review or your company's human resources department for additional insights.

5. Fit—Explore the person's best fit in the organization in light of his abilities, passions, and opportunities. Consider doors that are open now, those that require additional education or training, and those that might be available in the future on the same track. Also be honest enough to admit if no fit exists. There is every possibility that the company's goals in no way mesh with an individual's own aims in life. When that is the case, both the employee and the company are spinning their wheels. Remember that your job is to inspire others to live on purpose, but an employee in a situation like this is just "doing time.

6. Write a brief plan and schedule for each person to explore each of the elements in #2 through #5. List the resources you will bring to the discussions.

7 CREATE A NEW CULTURE

"There can be no transforming of darkness into light and of apathy into movement without emotion." – Carl Jung, *psychiatrist and author*

Before he coached UCLA, there had never been anyone like him. There probably never will be again.

College basketball junkies know that John Wooden's Bruins won ten national titles, including an unprecedented seven in a row from 1967 to 1973. Impressive—but his players know something even better than that. They know that John Wooden is far more than just a great coach—he is also a brilliant teacher, a caring mentor, a source of *inspiration*. In fact, according to former UCLA All-Star Bill Walton, of all of UCLA's great sports heroes, from Jackie Robinson to Kareem Abdul Jabbar, Coach Wooden surpasses them all in impact. Walton wrote, "John Wooden does not have the physical prowess that enables so many others to dominate their sports. Nor does he have a dominating, overwhelming personality to give him complete control over his world. What he has is a heart, brain, and soul that put him in a position to inspire others to reach levels of success and peace of mind that we could never dream of reaching by ourselves."[1]

Wooden's coaching style was understated, low-key. He never yelled or screamed at his players, and he never ranted at the officials. He also never asked his players to do anything that he wasn't already doing. And though every coach wants his team to *win*, Wooden's players never heard him utter the word. In fact, while many coaches were busy creating a high-pressure culture of rivalry, hostility, obsession, and success at any cost, Wooden was focusing simply on imparting character and teaching the fundamentals of the game. "And teach he did," wrote Walton, "everything as a matter of fact, on a constant basis. From showing us how to put our shoes and socks on, to how to get dressed properly so that our equipment and tools would never interfere with our goals and dreams, to how to build a foundation based on the human values and personal characteristics that are embodied in his pyramid of success so that when you aren't hot, when you are not in the zone, when the ball bounces the other way, you will still be able to achieve peak performance on command."[2] Coach Wooden created an environment in which players wanted to learn everything he could teach them. He made them thirsty to be the best they could be. In a phrase, he *built a new culture*.

"All of this was done in the subtlest of ways," Walton added. "While our practices were the most demanding endeavors that I've ever been a part of, so physically, emotionally, mentally and psychologically taxing, there is always the sense of joy, of celebration and of people having fun playing a simple game. Always positive, always constructive, John Wooden drives us in ways and directions that we are not aware of, always with the goal of making us better. It is never about him, never about the struggle for material accumulation, but always about individual skill and personal development within the framework of the team, the game and UCLA."[3]

Wooden is now an elderly man, and no one would argue that he was successful. His success as a coach speaks for itself. But his success as teacher and mentor is shown in the affection and admiration of those who played for him. He created perhaps the most powerfully positive culture of inspiration in the history of sports — and his players will never forget it.

DNA

Inspiring someone once is good, but it's only a start. For our affirmation to take root and have real impact, then, like Coach Wooden, we have to be consistent, tenacious, and creative. These things have to become part of our household's or organization's DNA, that is, their *culture*. Only then will employees, staff members, spouses, and children believe that we really mean what we say about their dreams and their abilities to reach them.

To create a corporate culture of inspiration, we, as leaders, first have to analyze our roles. Our task is to blend three things: *outcomes*, *people*, and *processes*. The *outcomes* are defined by company shareholders, executives above us, or perhaps by us. These are the external measurements of success consisting of production, share price, profits, and market share. Our conception of *people* can range from seeing them as cogs in our machine to sheep that we shepherd. Our perception of the organization's goals will determine the *processes* we use to organize people to accomplish those goals.

Each of us can see our role the way John Wooden envisioned his: as teachers committed to excellence and character development. Wooden wasn't just a cheerleader uttering empty slogans. As much as any leader, he valued outcomes, but he never used

We need to follow his example, making our home or workplace a culture of personal development.

people to accomplish self-centered goals. The development of individuals was every bit as important as winning basketball games. We need to follow his example, making our home or workplace a culture of *personal development*. Why? Because people who are developed to their fullest potential are *inspired* people. They are motivated to excel, and they will motivate others too.

INSPIRATION KILLERS

As you probably already know by comparing people's varied reactions to the same event, some folks thrive when the unexpected takes place; they simply improvise. But too much routine and a lack of variation from day to day squelch their personalities and stunt their inspiration. On the other hand, some people can't survive *without* a rigid, unchanging daily structure. When taken by surprise, they are crippled, and all inspiration is lost. In our role as teacher and coach of our employees (and children), we need to carefully observe the things that kill their inspiration. If we study the different profiles in the personality inventory in this book (or any other), we'll have a good idea both of what inspires people and what saps their enthusiasm.

Here's a synopsis of inspiration killers for each personality type:

— Commanders thrive on challenges, but they chafe when the goals are muddy, they get mixed messages from their leaders, or if others' expectations of them are too low. If you want to de-inspire a Commander, just try telling him he's not big enough for the "stage" when his heart was already set on being the "leading man."

— Coaches enjoy pulling a team together to accomplish tasks, but once the mission is accomplished, their enthusiasm will be crushed if the only ones thanked for a job well done are the team members. Obviously the team deserves to be appreciated for their efforts, but if you fail to acknowledge a Coach's contributions as well, then you have successfully put her inspiration to death. (Note: Coaches also suffer de-inspiration under rigid rules, lack of variety in assignments, or isolation from the group.)

— Innovators wilt under harsh criticism. They also don't do well under pressure to "hurry up and get 'er done." To keep an Innovator inspired, you'd better give him time to be creative — and then affirm him lavishly for his efforts. If he feels for even a moment that his contribution is not valued, his inspiration will drain as through a sieve.

— Accountability Partners, like Innovators, hate being rushed. Worse, they despise chaos, because Accountability Partners are *committed to excellence*. If you want to squash the inspiration of an Accountability Partner, then maintain a chaotic environment, where confusion rules and expectations are loosely defined. But if you want to inspire her to greatness, make sure that hers is an *ordered* environment where she is free to focus on systems, without distraction, and where attention to detail—especially hers—is valued.

In case you can't tell by now, I'm a Coach. I love working with people and getting to know them so that I can tailor my leadership to challenge them, affirm them, and provide structure or variety for them according to their specific need. I enjoy being thrown into complex situations, where I have to sort out people's goals and their relationships with each other. When I'm able to help them overcome roadblocks that have hindered them from being successful, I feel like a million dollars! But on those occasions when I feel alone and I have to follow a set of arbitrary and unnecessary rules, I become discouraged. My creativity evaporates, and my energy level dissipates. It's not a pretty sight.

Everybody on your team or in your family will eventually come in contact with an inspiration killer. We can't avoid every one. But we can be good students of those we lead so we can avoid crushing their spirits. Sometimes, rules must be followed, people have

> *Everybody on your team or in your family will eventually come in contact with an inspiration killer. We can't avoid every one. But we can be good students of those we lead so we can avoid crushing their spirits.*

to work alone, work is boring, and change upsets the status quo. But good leaders have built a culture of concern and trust. They have watched, listened, and identified the individual needs of their staff — and their staff know it. So even when inspiration tilts a little toward the downside, it doesn't take long to get everyone back on track.

But how *does* a leader build such a culture, a culture in which *every* member can be inspired to personal excellence?

BUILDING A CULTURE OF INSPIRATION: BE INTENTIONAL

Creating an inspiring culture doesn't just happen; it requires planning, discipline, and practice. But the first step is a ruthless commitment to *objectivity*. Some of us have tolerated the use of caustic words, attitudes, body language, and overtly negative actions so long that these destructive influences have become our DNA. They now spill not only out of us but also out of those who follow our example. Or perhaps we give mixed messages — sometimes appreciation, but often condemnation. We feel *so* good about the praise we give, but we discount the impact of the poison we sometimes excrete. Actually, psychologists tell us that mixed messages are even more powerfully manipulative than consistently negative ones, because mixed messages produce a toxic blend of hope and fear in others — the hope that they'll be praised and the fear that they'll be ridiculed or ignored.

The 360 Profile is a valuable tool to find out what kind of messages you communicate to the people around you. Let me encourage you to take the feedback with grace and humility. You may not like it, but don't disregard it. Instead, ask people to tell you more about their perceptions. Change can be difficult, but the best leaders know they have to make adjustments to be at their best and to create a culture in which others are at their best. To make changes, break them down into bite-sized chunks with manageable, measurable action steps. People who feel they have to change everything at once usually change nothing. Isolate the points of change (and we all can improve, even the best leaders among us), and prioritize them. Ask for assistance from a mentor, coach, or supervisor, and jump in with both feet. If it feels awkward at first, don't be alarmed. We felt awkward when we first learned to ride bikes as kids, but soon it became second nature. In the same way, new perceptions and skills will become second nature—part of the fabric of our DNA—as we practice them.

In the office, den, or bedroom, subtle shifts in the tone of conversation have dramatic results. We don't simply stop giving negative messages. Nature, as the physicists say, abhors a vacuum, so negative messages must be replaced with kindness, affirmation, vision, and hope. Even when people fail, our correction can inspire instead of destroy. We can say, "I'm confident this isn't your best work [or the kind of attitude you want to have]. I believe in you, and I know you can do better. I'll help anyway I can." Our words, though, aren't the only means of communication. Actually, words make up only 7 percent of communication. The impact of our tone of voice, facial features, and body language is even more important. We need to be aware of the look in our eyes as well as the words that come out of our mouths.

To radically change the culture and climate in your office and home, let me offer a few suggestions broadly, as well as the specifics of weekly and monthly planning.

Know your people.

Take some time to think about each person on your team, and jot down each one's personality profile. Notice the "inspiration killers" for each, and then identify the things you do and say that might kill his or her motivation. Also, list the person's strengths and needs according to the profile's description, and keep that information close at hand for the next month to remind you what to expect from each person and to tailor your communication to each in order to be most effective. After a month, this information should be ingrained in your mind. It will shape your interactions with people.

Know yourself.

How would you describe your leadership style up to this point? More importantly, how would your staff describe your leadership style? Is it:

- consultative, or commanding?
- confirming, or critical?
- clear, or cloudy?

Now, based on your personality profile, what are your greatest leadership strengths? What negative tendencies do you need to watch out for and overcome?

Prepare!

Before each staff meeting, do your homework. Find an appropriate story—your own or someone else's—that will inspire your team. (Review Principle #5 for preparation tips.) Then practice it, making sure you have a fitting conclusion that connects the dots for your listeners so that the story's lesson will be clear. Also consider the agenda for the meeting, and determine how you can best blend the organization's desired outcomes, the people involved, and the process for directing them to inspire them to excellence.

Notice, name, and nurture.

We talked about this at length in Principle #2, but it bears repeating.

Whether at home or in the conference room, as you get to know each person better, you'll find out what makes him or her tick. Notice each person's dreams and abilities, name them, and nurture them. You'll be amazed at how much it means to people when you take an extra minute or two to affirm them. It will transform the entire culture. Every person under your leadership will be more animated, more disciplined, and more effectual.

Build a team spirit.

Let's face it: Some people are extremely high-control leaders, and they expect people to jump when they say a single word. A few of them are powerful enough to actually command that kind of respect, but in the vast majority of cases when I've seen this demand in action, the leaders are just megalomaniacs who thrive on dominating others. It ain't pretty. Still, many of us, when we feel threatened, will raise our levels of control and demand compliance from those around us. But the more we feel comfortable in our own skins — authentic about our strengths and our weaknesses — the better able we will be to lower the demands and invite people to participate on a genuine team. Instead of mandating compliance, we will ask others to share their opinions — and here's the big deal: we don't become defensive if they disagree with us. I love to see secure leaders respond to a staff member who brings up a different point of view, by saying, "That's an interesting position. Tell me more about what you're thinking." In that environment, every person on the team feels included, energized, accepted — and inspired to do his or her best work. Best of all, the whole team will be more accepting of the varied views of its members. They will work better together — all because you have successfully fostered a team spirit.

One of the most effective team-building activities is something that I've implemented in staff meetings. I ask each of my staff to identify strengths in the team member

These lateral affirmations create very strong ties, smooth communications, and build a culture of loyalty.

on his or her right. In this way, inspiration doesn't just come from me. Over the years, I've watched these lateral affirmations create very strong ties, smooth communications, and build a culture of loyalty. (This is a wonderful activity to add to your weekly "Rose-Pinning Ceremony." See below.)

CHANGING THE CULTURE — IT'S A PROCESS

We love dramatic stories — like Indiana Jones, the Bourne trilogy, *Mission Impossible*, and anything featuring Bruce Willis. On a few occasions, as leaders have sought to build an inspiring culture, the stories were dramatic. I've personally witnessed *extraordinary* change. But more often, change happens more slowly. The Bible contains some of the most dramatic moments in all of literature, such as the parting of the Red Sea, or the little shepherd boy David killing the Philistine giant Goliath with a stone from a sling. When Jesus taught people about change, though, he often used agrarian metaphors. A farmer's work of tilling the soil and planting seed, and a *season* of warmth and rain, results in the harvest. It doesn't magically appear, and it doesn't come instantly. The harvest takes time and work, but eventually, diligent farmers are rewarded with a good harvest.

In my work at changing the culture of teams, divisions, companies, and families, I've found that most supervisors and spouses are thrilled with the efforts of those who diligently seek to build an inspiring culture. In fact, they've been hoping for these changes for a long time! But in a few, isolated instances, supervisors have resisted these changes and belittled managers for taking steps to build a team spirit. When that happens, I encourage these managers to keep inspiring their staff, but not to advertise it too broadly. Usually, the positive benefits the team experiences cause reluctant supervisors to admit that inspiring people is worth it after all. If insecure supervisors still condemn managers who are trying to motivate their staff, I encourage these managers to look for another place to serve. We just can't thrive (or even function) in that kind of oppressive environment.

On our teams, we can expect a range of responses to our efforts to change the culture. Various studies, including Everett M. Rogers's book, *Diffusion of Innovations,* identify reactions ranging from "early adopters" who internalize concepts quickly and become supportive of change almost from the outset, to "middle adopters," "late adopters," and those who resist change at all costs. We really appreciate staff members who nod when we're introducing new material and can't wait to implement it, but we shouldn't see these eager folks as the-norm. Most people are "from Missouri," and they require their leaders to "show me" before they get on board. A few hear the concept, see it modeled, and watch as the rest of the team implements the changes, but they refuse to budge until they are sure all the bugs have been worked out and there's no chance for failure. Thankfully, not many people in the workforce are late adopters, and at the far end of the spectrum, those who resist to the death don't last long in most companies!

You can change your culture. But remember, Rome wasn't built in a day . . .

You can *change* your culture. But remember, Rome wasn't built in a day . . .

Develop a weekly plan.

Some of us just let our weekly staff meetings happen. We do minimal planning, except to print out sales reports or something else we need to cover. But to create a culture of inspiration, we have to do better than that. We need to take a few minutes to craft a plan so that people leave staff meetings thinking, *Man, that was fantastic! I can't wait to get to work,* instead of, *Good grief. That was a waste of time.*

In your plan, consider these elements:

— **The Attention Grabber.** Begin your meeting with an arresting story about someone who did something courageous and noble.

— **"Show and Tell."** Ask different people to communicate one of their defining moments to the team. (These often take a while to share and digest, because they tap into people's emotions, so you may want to save this activity for longer, monthly meetings. Still, the weekly meeting may be a good time to preselect the next person to share his or her defining moment. This will give the individual time to think about ways to tell the story in a manner that will inspire the whole team.) These defining moments can be events from the distant past or simply everyday events that happen at work, both positive *and* negative. Encourage your team to be honest. Team members suffer if we create a climate that tells them they're in big trouble if they have dissatisfied clients. But if we promote the idea that difficult moments become life-changing lessons, then team members won't lie to each other or try to hide their struggles. When your people feel free to communicate their struggles and the lessons they learned in dealing with management or customers, *everybody* on the team benefits.

— **The Rose-Pinning Ceremony.** This activity comes in two parts. First, point out the strengths and contributions of at least one team member, maybe more, and be sure you share these affirmations equally as the weeks go by, so that every team member feels noticed and her strengths are named and nurtured.

The second part of this activity involves the *entire* team. Share the team's successes since the last meeting. My wife, Debbi, often tells stories about satisfied clients, full of specifics and quotes to highlight the contribution of each staff member.

These elements of a staff meeting aren't just fluff, and they aren't wasted time. They provide opportunities for members of the team to build bridges of understanding, and they provide insights about people and the work to be done, so that adjustments can be made in plans for the future. For example, as I get to know people's passions, I assign responsibilities more effectively, and I tailor the work to fit people's abilities. These seemingly minor alterations result in greater efficiency, higher productivity, fewer conflicts and misunderstandings, and more satisfied customers. That's not a bad outcome.

As time goes by, people will look forward to these staff meetings because they're convinced that these times together will be meaningful. A few minutes of preparation promise to produce inspiration and deeper connections among team members. Yes, it takes some time to prepare, and yes, it takes time to share these thoughts in the meeting. The question you have to ask is, "Is it worth it?" My answer, after watching the light come on in people's eyes over and over again, is, "You bet it is!"

Develop a monthly plan.

Changing a culture, particularly one infected with fear and negativity from the past, doesn't happen overnight. We can communicate a new direction in an instant, but people need time to let our new values soak in. They also need time to see if we really believe what we're saying and if we're committed to the changes we say we want to implement. I recommend that you schedule two hours with your team each month to cover a few specific topics that we've addressed in this book. You can use the "Going Deeper" exercises directly from the book, or you can download them from the Web site (www.inspirationblvd.com).

— **First month:** Introduce the concept of inspiration, share how this book and other resources have influenced your thinking, and explain that you want to spend time over the next few months to get to know each team member better so that all of them can be more inspired and effective than ever. Explain that this month you want to ask a few questions about the team's vision for making a positive impact on others. Then ask:

  - How is our company [or nonprofit organization, church, or family] making a difference in people's lives?
  - How is our team contributing to this effort? What are we doing well? In what areas do we need to improve?
  - How is each of us contributing to this effort? In what aspects of work do you feel most fulfilled? In what aspects do you feel most frustrated?
  - What difference would it make if each of us individually and all of us as a team aligned our dreams and abilities with the company's goals?

— **Second month:** Before the meeting, have staff members complete the Inspiration Personality Profile on paper or online, and have them bring the results to the meeting. There, ask people to:

- Tell the results of the inventory, including the analysis of the strengths and needs.
- Explain how accurate (or inaccurate) they believe the profile is for them.
- Discuss the specifics of what motivates them on the job and what kills their inspiration.
- Share the insights they've learned about each other after they've heard team members explain their inventories.

— **Third month:** Before the meeting, explain (in person or in an e-mail) the concept of "defining moments" as "ones that stop us in our tracks and cause us to reevaluate our direction in life." Ask people to prepare for the meeting by completing the exercise asking these questions:

- Identify the most difficult moments or periods of your life.
- Are these your "defining moments" that taught you life's most important lessons? Why or why not?
- What happened?
- How did they affect you at the time?
- What lessons did you learn then, or what lessons do you see now that you look back at those events?
- Identify the difficult moments at work (with management or clients) in the last few weeks. How have these affected you? What lessons did you learn, or what lessons do you need to learn from those events?

In the meeting, share your defining moment first, and then ask people to share theirs. You probably don't want to *require* people to share their experiences. It's better to *invite* them, giving them an "out" if they don't feel comfortable telling these things to the group. Trust often takes time to grow. Your own openness, coupled with a lack of pressure, will provide a positive, healthy environment.

— **Fourth month:** Assign team members the "Going Deeper" exercise at the end of Principle #2 about uncovering dreams. In the meeting, share yours first, and then invite others to share theirs. Be careful not to judge anyone's dream. Affirm as much as you can, and at least appreciate people's willingness to share their hearts with the group. Use "tell me more about it" to show your interest and to elicit more insight and discussion.

— **Fifth month:** At least two weeks before the next meeting, assign the 360 Profile. Your staff will need this time to go online and set it up. Again, take the initiative in the meeting and share your insights from the exercise; then invite others to share their discoveries. For the profile, they will have gotten input from several people on the team, and some of it may not have been overwhelmingly positive. Make sure this is an affirming, uplifting conversation.

— **Sixth month:** Assign the "Think about it . . ." section from Principle #6, about purpose. In the meeting, explain the process you've experienced in clarifying your own sense of purpose, and invite others on the team to share their insights and process.

These six months of reflection and discussion should provide a wealth of insights for you as the leader and for each person on the team. In most cases, people will feel understood — one of the most important components of mental health and teamwork. When people feel understood, stress levels go down, motivation goes up, and everyone excels at work and in relationships. Invariably, team leaders will find that a few people on the team are gifted storytellers, so when the leaders need to make a report to the division exec, they can call on one of these gifted staff members to craft a story to tell.

When new people join the team, be sure to help each person get up to speed with the culture of the team by completing these exercises and having existing team members share their dreams, abilities, and purpose with the new staff.

As much as possible, reach deep into the organizational structure to connect with employees and create an inspiring culture. If you are a top executive, talk to people all the way down to the mailroom to tell them your story. Ask them about their defining moments and the lessons they learned, and share their stories in your staff meetings. In fact, you might want to ask one of them to come to your staff meetings from time to time to talk about how they turned a difficult encounter with a customer, client, or vendor into a lesson for a lifetime. Your interaction with them speaks volumes about your priorities of people before profits, and it sets a terrific example for the rest of your team to treat their staff and clients with respect and serve them with excellence.

If you have followed this six-month plan, then you have invested *half a year* in creating a culture of inspiration. But don't stop there. Keep learning, keep growing, and keep developing your skills. If you will continue to implement the suggestions in this chapter, your team will be glad you did, and so will you. You will *all* be inspired. What's more, as you cultivate an inspiring culture for *your* team, other teams will sit up and take notice. They'll follow your example! And best of all, if you can create this kind of culture at *work*, you can do it at home, too, with your spouse and your children.

A FINAL THOUGHT: CHANGING THE CULTURE AT HOME

Our interactions shape us. The messages we give and receive from one another are mirrors that reflect our identity. Our reflection in the mirrors consists of the messages we've received from parents, siblings, teachers, bosses, and friends. For some of us, the mirrors we've looked into are like the ones I used to see at county fairs that distorted our images. One made me look really tall and skinny, another made me look short and fat, and a third one made me look as if I had the worst case of scoliosis in history! If I believed that's actually how I looked, I'd be really discouraged. In the same way, some of us have absorbed negative messages that have given us distorted images of ourselves. Creating a culture of inspiration isn't based on empty promises and phony affirmations. It's based on rock-hard reality and the identification of a person's dreams, abilities, and purpose. As we are honest and affirming, we offer new, positive mirrors for people to look into. They'll like what they see! The images of truth and acceptance may be new to them, but gradually, they'll learn to live by those new images and messages. They'll believe that their dreams are important, that they have valuable abilities, and that they can make a difference — a big difference — in other people's lives. Sure, they have room for improvement, but in an atmosphere of affirmation, they can listen to truth, even hard truth, far more easily. Make yours a culture of inspiration. If you've failed up to now, here's a little story . . . to *inspire* you.

Not long ago, I was in a seminar with a number of colleagues. As we discussed the power of affirming people for who they are even more than for what they do, I looked over at my friend Wade. He had tears in his eyes. I asked him to tell us what he was thinking and feeling, and he told us, "I've just realized that I've made a huge mistake parenting my two sons. One of them is a gifted athlete and a good student. He gets praise from teachers, coaches, and from me. But my other son struggles with just about everything in his life. He plays sports, but not as well as his brother. He doesn't do very well in school, and he isn't as popular as my other son." Wade took a deep breath, wiped the tears from his eyes, and then continued. "Virtually all of my communication with my younger son is corrective. I'm always on his case, pointing out what he's done wrong. In this meeting as we've been talking, I realize what I'm doing to him." Then Wade looked up at each of us as he said with conviction,

"I'm going to change that—starting today. As of this min-ute, I will make it my life's mission to affirm my dear son for who he is—loved, precious, and dear to me. I'm going home *today* to tell him how much I appreciate his character and his heart, and I'm going to say a lot less about the things he doesn't do so well."

Wade's relationship with his son changed that day. In fact, the whole at-home culture changed to one of affirma-tion and inspiration—and neither Wade nor his son will ever be the same.

And that's the way it is. Lives are changed for good—when in-spiration's in the house!

THINK ABOUT IT . . .

1. Who is someone you've known who is most like Coach Wood-en? What kind of impact did (or does) that person have on people, including you?

2. What do you think it means to "create a culture of inspiration"? What might that look like?

3. How do you normally respond to change? Are you an early adopter, middle adopter, late ("show me") adopter, or "over my dead body" (never) adopter? Explain your answer.

4. What are some "inspiration killers" for you? Can you identify them for the people in your family and on your team? If so, what are they?

5. What is one thing you can do today to create more of an inspiring environment for people around you?

6. What can you do to bring "inspiration in the house"?

GOING DEEPER

1. Know your people.
   - Take some time to think about each person on your team, and jot down each person's personality profile.

   - List the person's strengths and needs according to the profile's description, and keep that information close at hand for the next month to remind you what to expect from each person and to tailor your communication to be most effective.

2. Know yourself.
   - How would you describe your leadership style up to this point?

— More importantly, how would your staff describe your leadership style? Is it consultative or commanding, confirming or critical, clear or cloudy?

— Based on your personality profile, what are your greatest leadership strengths?

— What negative tendencies do you need to watch out for and overcome?

3. Prepare!
   Before your next staff meeting, do your homework. Find an appropriate story — your own or someone else's — that will inspire your team. Then practice it, making sure you have a fitting conclusion that connects the dots for your listeners so that the story's lesson will be clear. Also consider the agenda for the meeting, and determine whether you can effectively blend the organization's desired outcomes, the people involved, and the process for directing them and motivating them to excel.

4. Write out a six-month plan to create a culture of inspiration for your team. You can use the suggestions in this chapter, and you may want to add additional resources. Be sure to put the preparation phase for each exercise in the schedule to give people time to complete them.

5. How do you hope these six months will affect your team, each person on the team, and you as the leader?

6. List the important relationships you've had in your life, and describe the messages you've received from these "mirrors."

7. List the important relationships in your life today. Describe the images they have gotten from looking at you (as a mirror) in the last several months.

8. Next to each one, describe the images and messages you want to reflect to each one in the next few days, weeks, and months.

9. Write a simple plan for how you want to communicate those messages. Which three will you focus on first?

Conclusion:
The Courage to Inspire

"A hero is no braver than an ordinary man, but he is braver five minutes longer." – Ralph Waldo Emerson

In 1924, British climber George Mallory was asked why he wanted to climb Mt. Everest, the tallest and most daunting mountain in the world and which, at the time, had never been climbed. Mallory replied with eloquent simplicity, "Because it's there." In the past century, climbing the most treacherous peaks in the world has become an obsession for a few brave men and women. They don't climb for fame or fortune. They climb to challenge themselves to reach for more than they've ever achieved before, to push past the limits of physical and psychological endurance, to stare death in the face—and take another step.

At the young age of 21, Stacy Allison caught the bug. On her first major climb on Mt. Huntington in Alaska, she was only 200 feet from the summit when her partner's ice ax broke. They turned around, brokenhearted but even more determined to reach the top of as many peaks as possible. She reflected, "Our ability to respond positively to setbacks, fuels our creativity and lays the foundation for future successes."

The next year, Stacy reached the top of Mt. McKinley, the tallest mountain on the continent of North America, and she participated with a team of women who climbed Nepal's 22,495-foot peak, Ama Dablam. These feats, though, were only preparation for the ultimate challenge: Mt. Everest. She joined the North Face Expedition, but she failed to reach the top. She and her fellow climbers were caught in the worst storm on the mountain in 40 years, and they were trapped in a snow cave for five days at 23,500 feet. Again, she faced the reality of failure to attain a goal that had extracted a high price in time, effort, and money. Stacy learned a valuable lesson from this disappointment. She wrote, "If you see yourself as trying to beat the mountain, eventually the mountain will win. You don't conquer mountains; you cooperate with them."

She returned to Mt. Everest with a different team, the Northwest American Everest Expedition, and after climbing from base camp to base camp for 29 days and a final push to the top, Stacy became the first American woman to reach the top of the world at 29,028 feet.

Stacy led teams up the slopes of K2, thought by many to be the most difficult mountain in the world to climb. As a leader, she valued each person as much or more than the goal of reaching the summit. On one of these expeditions, three of the seven members of the team reached the top, but injury to one necessitated that the entire team call off the climb and head back down.

Tens of thousands of people hike stretches of the Appalachian Trail every year, and tens of thousands more hike paths in the Rockies, the Cascades, and other ranges across the country. Mountain climbing, however, is categorically different. Mistakes on hiking trails lead to blisters; mistakes on Everest can end in death. The few, dedicated climbers who attempt the world's highest peaks endure grueling training and invest significant portions of their lives and finances to participate in an expedition. When they finally arrive in Nepal or Tibet, they don't get off the plane and hike to the top. They face weeks, if not months, of additional preparations, securing resources and assistance and setting up one base camp after another. The elevations are so difficult on the human body that climbers have to become acclimated to each camp for several days before they can make the next ascent. The effort, expense, and tenacity pay off in stories of triumph and tragedy. Those who climb to the top of the world experience excruciating moments of self-doubt and conflict with team members about decisions made by oxygen-starved brains. Still, these men and women are driven to try to achieve what few others have dared. They know they may fail, but that doesn't stop them. In fact, nothing—except weather, injury, or death—will stop them. That's the essence of their courage.

The lessons Stacy Allison learned in climbing translate to every arena in life. Stacy has written two books, *Beyond The Limits: A Woman's Triumph on Everest* and *Many Mountains to Climb: Reflections on Competence, Courage and Commitment*. These books recount her experiences in climbing the most perilous mountains in the world, and she explains the principles she applies to overcoming every struggle in our lives. The difficulties we all face, she is certain, will make or break us. As a philosopher wrote, "What doesn't kill us makes us stronger." Stacy reflected on her role as a team builder, "In any endeavor, leaders should inspire members of the team with a passion for success, but within the framework of team effort. One of the most crucial things to realize, feel and remember, is that when one team member succeeds, the entire team succeeds."

> *"In any endeavor, leaders should inspire members of the team with a passion for success, but within the framework of team effort. One of the most crucial things to realize, feel and remember, is that when one team member succeeds, the entire team succeeds."*

THE CHALLENGE OF LEADERSHIP

In the introduction, I promised that if you apply even one of the seven principles in this book, you'll see very positive change. And it's true. Just one principle will, as I put it, "move the needle forward in your ability to inspire others." Of course, the more principles you apply, the more changes you can expect, but if you want to start small and add more later, that's fine. The important thing is that you start—right where you are. Some of you will . . . but some of you won't.

When men and women in executive and management positions tell me, "I just can't inspire people," they've got it all wrong. No one is asking them to forsake their God-given personality to become something they're not. Instead, I'm asking them to become all they can be in relationships, to learn a few basic principles and apply them at work and at home. Can they do that? Of course they can. I know. I've seen men and women muster the courage to take steps to change their perceptions and behaviors. In most cases, these steps were small, but they produced major benefits.

Some who read this book will embrace the seven principles, bind themselves to them like glue, and use them zealously to inspire everyone with whom they come in contact to greatness. Yet others will start out with the best of intentions—then drop the ball, as others have before them. And some won't try at all.

Why *do* some people rise to the challenge of inspiring people but others don't? There may be a complicated matrix of reasons, but at the core it's not primarily a lack of experience, training, or personality—it's the lack of *courage*. Without courage, all the skills in the world are underutilized. They lie dormant—because of fear.

Fears are validated by excuses. We tell ourselves that there are *good reasons* why we don't "reach out" and inspire someone. Here are just a few I've heard (some that I've used myself) that attempt to validate resistance to change:

- "I'm too busy to think about it."
- "I'm under too much pressure from the boss to take time to learn 'inspiration principles.'"
- "Inspire people? It's just not me."
- "I'd like to spend time motivating my staff, but they just don't respond to that kind of thing quickly enough."
- "My employees don't appreciate me. They're not worth it."

— "I'd come across as phony."

— "I don't want to expose myself to people any more than I have to."

— "I don't know how."

— "I'm confused."

— "I'm not a good speaker."

— "That's just too much to add to our staff meeting. Our stockholders don't pay us to hold hands and feel good about ourselves."

— "If my boss knew I was spending time trying to inspire my staff, I'd be fired today."

Excuses, excuses. And the one I've heard the most is the classic, "I don't want to look stupid." Maybe you feel the same way. Perhaps stereotypes fill your mind. They are certainly a part of our lives. When we think of NFL quarterbacks, we think of Brett Favre, Tom Brady, or Peyton Manning. When we think of rich people, we think of Bill Gates and Warren Buffett. When we think of the most beautiful couples, we think of — well, we probably shouldn't put the names of couples, because they may not still be married by the time this gets into print. But in the same way, when we think of inspiring people, we often think of high-profile, over-the-top people, like Tony Robbins and Zig Ziglar. They're gifted and effective, true — but you don't have to receive a DNA transplant from one of these people to be an inspiring leader! And no one is asking you to become something you're not. Instead, I'm asking you to learn a few basic principles and to begin to apply them at work and at home to build an inspiring culture. Can you do that?

Of course you can. I've seen men and women muster the courage to take steps, one by one, to overcome their fear and create a culture of inspiration. In most cases, these steps were small, yet they produced major benefits. They'll do the same for you, but only to the extent that your level of desperation surpasses your level of fear. Until then, you will cling to the familiar and forfeit the prospects of progress.

NEXT STEPS

At some point, though, all of us need to step back, take a good look at our lives, and ask if we're valuing the right things. Do we live to avoid conflict? Do we value placating our boss more than caring for our staff? Is self-protection our highest virtue? Or are we willing to call a spade a spade, step out, take a risk, and try to make a difference in someone's life?

You're willing to risk it, you say? OK, then let's get started. Pick a principle—*any* principle. Here they are for your quick review.

1. Start being real—today! Take off your mask and be authentic—from now on!

2. Look around you. Who's got a dream? Connect with that individual—just him or her, to start—and watch the inspiration begin to swell.

3. Begin looking for someone's hidden abilities—I dare you! And when you find them, name them and nurture them. That person will stand a little taller from this time forth.

4. Make a decision—right now!—to be credible in every way. Shed any pretense and be honest at all times. People are inspired by those they can trust.

5. Tell a good story—this very night—to your tired spouse who's had a hard day, a friend who's down in the dumps, or your kid who came home with two Ds on his report card. Do you have something to say that will inspire this loved one? I bet you do.

6. Pick someone—anyone—who needs help living life on *purpose;* then dedicate yourself to helping him find the purpose that he needs to live out. And finally,

7. Change your culture—beginning with you. Watch the words that come out of your mouth. If they are edifying and affirming, by all means, say them. But if they're just critical and condemning, bite your tongue. Do this a few times and it will become natural to only let the good come out. And when the good outweighs the bad, believe me, the climate will *change.*

That wasn't so hard, was it? Practicing just one principle is like throwing a rock into a motionless lake. That rock (you!) will come in contact with one person . . . but it doesn't stop there. Watch for the ripple. It'll move outward toward shore. The person you impact will impact others—but only if *you* make the first move.

Go ahead, be that rock that starts the ripple effect—*today.*

What's in It for You?

When we finally get the courage to take steps forward, it is perhaps we who are most affected. As we help others identify their dreams, ours come into sharper focus. When we notice, name, and nurture others' abilities, we craft our leadership skills. As we try to enrich others with great stories and defining moments from our own lives, our lives become immeasurably richer because others tell us stories of failure and courage. Instead of the constant stress of trying to force people to be successful so we look good, we can relax, devote ourselves to helping them align their desires with the company's goals, and stand back and watch the powerfully positive chemical reaction. At the end of each day, we go home and build into our spouses and children in the same way, loving them, affirming them, listening to them, and helping them soar. And we sleep soundly, knowing our lives *really* matter.

Think about it . . .

1. What are some fears and excuses that you've heard from people who didn't want to implement change? What are some you've used?

2. What are your expectations as you think of implementing the seven principles in this book? Do you expect instantaneous or gradual change to occur? Explain your answer.

3. What's the next step for you?

4. What difference will your implementation of these principles make in your team at work and in your family a month from now, six months from now, and a year from now?

GOING DEEPER

1. Describe the most courageous leader you've ever known personally.

2. What impact did that person have on you?

3. What would your best friends and closest coworkers say are your fears and excuses? How do these "work" for you?

4. Who are some people in your company or in your family who would benefit from understanding and applying the seven principles in this book?

NOTES

Acknowledgments

1. C. S. Lewis, *The Problem of Pain* (New York: Macmillan, 1944; New York: HarperCollins, 2001), 93. Citations are to the Harper Collins edition.

Introduction

1. Dictionary.com, v. 1.1, s.v. "Inspiring," http://dictionary.reference.com/search?q=inspiring&db=* (accessed May 7, 2008).
2. Jim Collins, *Good to Great: Why Some Companies Make the Leap . . . and Others Don't* (New York: Harper Business, 2001), 20.
3. Ibid., 45–46.

Principle #1

1. David S. Broder, "Three Words for the Next President," *Washington Post,* November 22, 2007, A37, http://www.washingtonpost.com/wp-dyn/content/article/2007/11/21/AR2007112101860.html?sub=AR.
2. Carl Castaneda on Wisdom Quotes, Copyright © 1995–2006 Jone Johnson Lewis, http://www.wisdomquotes.com/003332.html.

Principle#2

1. Dr. Richard Swenson, *Margin: Restoring Emotional, Physical, Financial and Time Reserves to Our Overloaded Lives* (Colorado Springs: Navpress, 2004).
2. John Ortberg, "Diagnosing Hurry Sickness," *Leadership,* Fall 1998.
3. Stephen Covey on the Zenhabits Web site, "Exclusive Interview: Stephen Covey on His Morning Routine, Blogs,

Technology, GTD and The Secret," http://zenhabits. net/2008/02/exclusive-interview-stephen-covey-on-his-morning-routine-blogs-technology-gtd-and-the-secret/. See also Stephen R. Covey, *The 7 Habits of Highly Effective People: Powerful Lessons in Personal Change* (New York: Free Press, 2004).

4. Robert Lewis, *Authentic Manhood: Winning at Work and Home* (DVD Kit and Workbook) (Nashville: Lifeway), 2005.

Principle #3

1. Winston S. Churchill, "Sir Winston Churchill: The Man, His Life, and His Archive" (address to the Yushodo Forum, Waseda University, May 15, 2002, http://yushodo.co.jp/pinus/53/forum/churc1/eng2.html).

2. William Manchester, *The Last Lion: Alone* (New York: Dell, 1988), 236.

3. Winston Churchill, *The Gathering Storm* (New York: Bantam Books/Houghton Mifflin, 1948), 196.

4. Sarah Chana Radcliffe, "The Positive-Negative Ratio," www. aish.com/family/mensch/The_Positive_-_Negative_Ratio. asp.

5. Rodd Wagner and James K. Harter, The Elements of Great Managing (New York: Gallup Press, 2006), 52.

Principle #4

1. Gene Smith, *Lee and Grant* (New York: McGraw Hill, 1984), 295.

2. Stephen M. R. Covey, *The Speed of Trust* (New York: Free Press, Simon & Schuster, 2006), 14. Covey notes that when trust deteriorates, the speed of business slows down and costs increase. He calls this the "trust tax."

Principle #5

1. Flannery O'Connor, *Mystery and Manners* (New York: Farrar, Straus & Giroux, 1961), 118.

2. Howard Gardner in Tom Peters, *Leading Minds* (New York: DK London, Munich, Melbourne, and Delhi, 2005), 78.
3. Peters, *Leading Minds.*

Principle #6
1. Os Guinness, *The Call* (Nashville: Word, 1998), 4.
2. John Lewis in "A 'Dream' Remembered," *NewsHour,* August 28, 2003.

Principle #7
1. "John Wooden—Like UCLA—Simply the Best," www.billwalton.com/wooden.html.
2. Ibid.
3. Ibid.

ABOUT THE AUTHOR

Terry Barber is Vice President and Senior Strategist for the Grizzard Communication Group, and primarily serves the nonprofit healthcare segment as well as colleges and universities in the area of philanthropic branding, including a number of NCI-designated Cancer Centers and major medical centers.

Over the past 15 years, Terry has provided brand and fundraising consulting for many of the Children's Miracle Network affiliated Hospitals, Texas A&M Alumni Association, Ouachita Baptist University Admissions Counseling, and the child sponsorship agencies, Compassion International and World Vision.

Terry and Benny

In the fall of 1987, Terry started and managed a nonprofit company that focused on helping teens develop positive, principle-based self-esteem. This provided the opportunity to serve hundreds of schools nationwide and to personally speak to over 500,000 students in assembly and classroom settings. He also has written and produced a six-part video curriculum that was used in over 600 school districts around the United States.

Most recently, Terry created a web 2.0 initiative called Inspiration Blvd., LLC, and he holds the title of Chief Inspirational

Terry and Debbi

Terry's four daughters

Officer (http://www.inspirationblvd.com). The web site is capturing the attention and imagination of people interested in inspiring others as well as being inspired.

As a popular speaker for corporate training and events, and an inspirational resource to the nonprofit community, he speaks each week somewhere in the country on "Raising the Inspiration Factor," "How to Be an Inspiring Leader," and "How to Use Story-telling to Connect with Others."

Terry holds a Masters Degree from New Orleans Baptist Seminary and continues to be actively involved in his passion for an orphanage in Uganda, Africa, and Child Sponsorship and Early Childhood Education in Guatemala.

He resides in Alpharetta, Georgia, and is married to Debbi. He is proud of his four daughters and three grandchildren.

Inspiration^{SM} Boulevard

If you lead people, you need this site!

Inspiration Boulevard is highly interactive and provides a wide array of tools to help you inspire the people around you. Before every staff meeting, go online and find a great story to tell them.

In addition, Inspiration Boulevard:

— Invites you to post your own story to inspire others.

— Lets you honor people who have inspired you.

— Find people who experienced difficult situations in life and are better people for it. You can connect with these people. (Inspiration Boulevard is "the Facebook of Inspiration"!)

— Helps you research, prepare and deliver inspiring talks.

— Provides downloadable tools to use for self-development or for your team.

— Connects you with one-on-one coaching opportunities.

— Enables you to schedule seminars, workshops, and seminars to raise the inspiration factor for your business and your church.

For more information, go to www.inspirationblvd.com today or contact Terry at tbarber@inspirationblvd.com

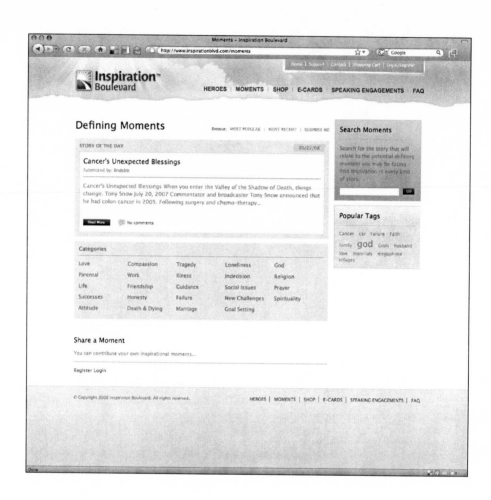

http://www.inspirationblvd.com/moments

Google

Inspiration™
Boulevard

Home | Support | Contact | Shopping Cart | Log-in/Register

HEROES | MOMENTS | SHOP | E-CARDS | SPEAKING ENGAGEMENTS | FAQ

Defining Moments

Browse: MOST POPULAR | MOST RECENT | SURPRISE ME

STORY OF THE DAY   10/22/08

Cancer's Unexpected Blessings
Submitted by: lindsbb

Cancer's Unexpected Blessings When you enter the Valley of the Shadow of Death, things change. Tony Snow July 20, 2007 Commentator and broadcaster Tony Snow announced that he had colon cancer in 2005. Following surgery and chemo-therapy...

Read More   No comments

Categories

Love	Compassion	Tragedy	Loneliness	God
Parental	Work	Illness	Indecision	Religion
Life	Friendship	Guidance	Social Issues	Prayer
Successes	Honesty	Failure	New Challenges	Spirituality
Attitude	Death & Dying	Marriage	Goal Setting	

Search Moments

Search for the story that will relate to the potential defining moment you may be facing - find inspiration in every kind of story.

GO

Popular Tags

Cancer car Failure Faith
family god Gods husband
love materials megaphone
villages

Share a Moment

You can contribute your own inspirational moments...

Register Login

HEROES | MOMENTS | SHOP | E-CARDS | SPEAKING ENGAGEMENTS | FAQ

To Order More Copies

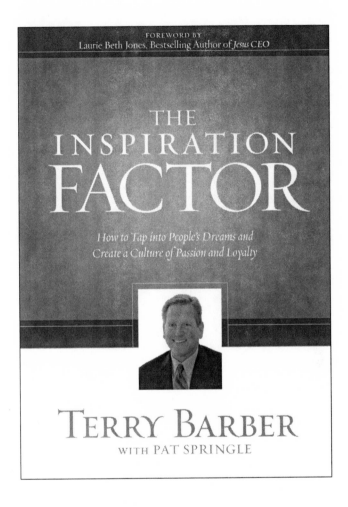

To order more books and find out discount
and shipping information, go to . . .

www.inspirationblvd.com

Printed in the United States
131802LV00004B/4/P